Students' Sense of Belonging and Involvement in College

Students' Sense of Belonging and Involvement in College

Key Insights from Research for Practice

Edited by
Terrell L. Strayhorn

BLOOMSBURY ACADEMIC
NEW YORK • LONDON • OXFORD • NEW DELHI • SYDNEY

BLOOMSBURY ACADEMIC
Bloomsbury Publishing Inc, 1359 Broadway, New York, NY 10018, USA
Bloomsbury Publishing Plc, 50 Bedford Square, London, WC1B 3DP, UK
Bloomsbury Publishing Ireland, 29 Earlsfort Terrace, Dublin 2, D02 AY28, Ireland

First published in the United States of America 2026

Cover design by Kathi Ha
Cover image © stellalevi/DigitalVision Vectors/Getty Images

Library of Congress Cataloging-in-Publication Data is available

ISBN: HB: 978-1-5381-8218-5
PB: 978-1-5381-8219-2
ePDF: 979-8-7651-5502-8
eBook: 978-1-5381-8220-8

Typeset by Deanta Global Publishing Services, Chennai, India
Printed and bound in the United States of America

For product safety related questions contact productsafety@bloomsbury.com.

To find out more about our authors and books visit www.bloomsbury.com and sign up for our newsletters.

For my father, Wilber Earl Strayhorn (10/31/1946–02/13/2025), who taught me timeless lessons about life, patience, love, and belonging. Belonging was his way of being. Being and becoming are the core of this book.

Contents

Foreword

Belonging is a basic human need. Need becomes practice when colleges commit to conditions where students feel seen, valued, and invited into meaningful involvement. Practice becomes promise when that involvement opens doors to relationships, learning, and leadership that last. For more than two decades, Professor Terrell L. Strayhorn has helped us measure that need, sharpen that practice, and realize that promise. Promise becomes pathways in these pages, where scholars and practitioners translate evidence into action for today's richly diverse student populations. From students with disabilities to LGBTQIA+ athletes, from HBCU communities to religiously affiliated students and many others, contributors illuminate what belonging looks like, how it feels, and why it matters. What matters here is not a slogan but a strategy: design for inclusion, measure what you value, and value what you measure. May this volume guide your next conversation, your next program, and your next courageous change.

Preface

Origins of the Project

Sense of belonging is a basic need and human right. That understanding led to questions about who feels they belong in college—and who does not. Questions led to research as I listened to students on campuses across the country and around the world describe the quiet power of a warm greeting, the cold sting of exclusion, and the catalytic role of involvement in organizations, classes, teams, and faith communities. Research and wonder led to this book—a curated set of chapters written by scholar-practitioners committed to evidence-based praxis.

Context and Trend

Belonging sits at the intersection of access, equity, and student success. Success today is not accidental—it is designed through policies, programs, pedagogy, and places that invite participation. Participation is trending upwards as institutions respond to demographic shifts, mental-health needs, digital learning, and calls for justice. Justice requires attention to students too often overlooked—those with disabilities, LGBTQIA+ athletes, HBCU communities, religiously affiliated students, adult learners, commuters, and more.

> "If involvement is the engine, belonging is the fuel."

Why This Book and Why Now

Campuses need a clear, inclusive playbook for enacting student success through belonging. Playbooks work when they blend research, theory, tools, and stories. Stories humanize data, data inform decisions, decisions shape daily experiences. Period. Transformative experiences accumulate into positive outcomes like class attendance, retention, persistence, thriving, and, yes, degree completion. This book meets a practical need: actionable guidance you can use on Monday morning, revisit during Wednesday's staff meeting, and measure (again) by Friday.

Goals of the Book

Readers will gain language, lenses, and learnings from high-quality, rigorous research studies that provide clear implications for campus involvement. This is important as language clarifies what we mean by belonging and involvement. Lenses, on the other hand, focus attention on identity, history, intersectionality, and universal design for diverse learners. Leveraging learning mobilizes leadership to change policies, redesign programs, and recalibrate assessment systems. Ultimately, I hope this book instills courage to do the next right thing for all students—especially those for whom college was not originally designed.

Intended Audiences and Uses

This book serves student affairs professionals, academic leaders, faculty, coaches, advisors, chaplains, disability services, institutional researchers, and governing boards. It suits graduate seminars, professional learning communities, cabinet retreats, and periodic assessment cycles, especially those that are part of institutional accreditation efforts. Cycles become culture when teams use insights from these chapters to run pilot studies, evaluate innovative programs, and co-create sustainable solutions with students.

Approach and Organization

The volume uses a design-for-belonging framework that integrates psychological theory, organizational change, and equity-minded assessment. Assessment informs action, action invites involvement, involvement strengthens belonging—forming a virtuous cycle (see Figure 0.1).

Chapters at a Glance

1. Introduction
2. Generation Covid and the College Experience: Exploring the Reverberations of 2020 on Young People's Transition and Engagement
3. "I'm More Than an Athlete": Exploring Sense of Belonging in College for Black LGBTQ+ Student-Athletes
4. "They Just So Happen to Be Born in the Right Family": A Story of Elitism on an HBCU Campus: Students' Sense of Belonging and Involvement in College
5. Toward Beloved Communities on Campus: Understanding the Intersections of Race, Gender, and Sexual Identity in Sense of Belonging Research as a Tool for Rethinking Campus Resources
6. Centering Relationships: Belongingness in the Context of Religious, Spiritual, and Secular Identities, Perceptions, and Experiences
7. The Conditional Effects of Participating in a Student Organization on College Students' Sense of Belonging
8. The Trifecta: The WHOLE Student Experience, Sense of Belonging, and Historically Black Colleges & Universities (HBCUs)
9. Black College Men with Disabilities Involvement On- and Off-Campus: Critical Insights for Policy, Practice and Future Research
10. Epilogue

"We don't measure belonging to admire numbers; we measure it to move them."

Case Study: The Tuesday Night Team

Context: Mid-size public university, commuter-heavy, low club participation among first-year students with disabilities.

Challenge: Students report feeling "unknown" and "in the way," avoiding evening events.

Intervention: Disability Services, Student Affairs, and Campus Recreation co-create Tuesday Night Team—universally designed, low-barrier involvement series (adaptive intramurals, makerspace hours, peer-led study pods).

Belonging Moves: Personalized invites, name-learning rituals, choice of roles, sensory-friendly spaces, transportation vouchers.

Assessment: Weekly check-ins, attendance records, brief belonging scale, focus groups after six weeks.

Results (Pilot): Attendance +62 percent, organization membership +29 percent, belonging scale ↑ 0.6 SD, help-seeking +35 percent, persistence to spring +4pp vs. matched controls.

Transferable Insight: Start with one night, one team, one set of inclusive moves. Scale by interest, not assumption.

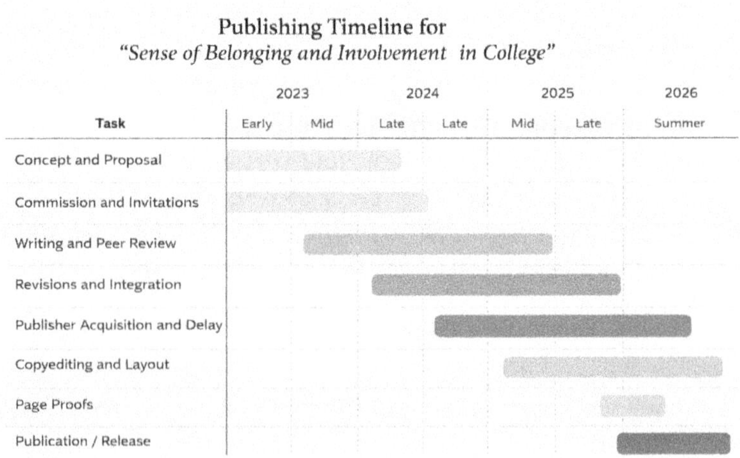

Figure 0.1 Assembly of the book: Gantt timeline (2023–6).

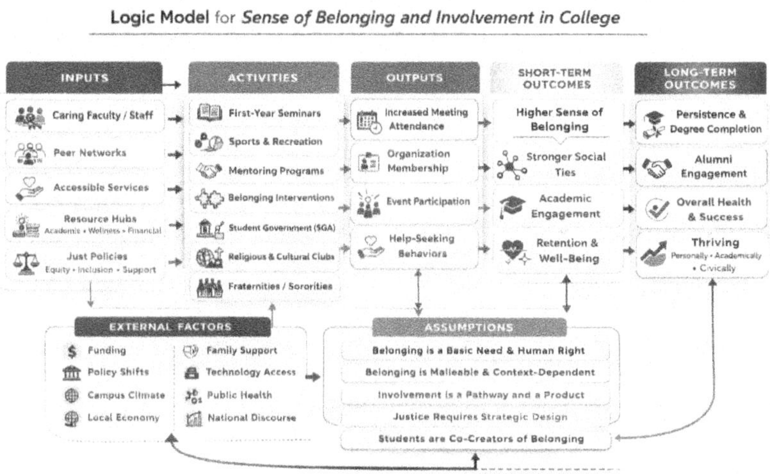

Figure 0.2 Logic Model: From belonging supports to involvement and outcomes.

Acknowledgments

Books are built *in* community. Community formed the scaffolding for this project from idea to page proofs. I am grateful to my staff and research team at Do Good Work Consulting Group, who gathered data, designed tools, and kept our shared values at the center of every survey, interview, pilot, and transcript, which allowed me "mental bandwidth" to lead, learn, and write. Centering values was also the commitment of faculty, staff, and students within the Evelyn Reid Syphax School of Education at Virginia Union University where I serve as Interim Dean, whose encouragement and wise counsel fueled each chapter. Chapters took shape because colleagues within Academic Affairs—including the Provost's Office—granted the time and space necessary to do the work well. Doing the work well depended on the contributing authors, whose scholarship and patience are the beating heart of this volume as it navigated a thorny production process during a publisher acquisition. Acquisition turned into acceleration thanks to the dedicated editorial team at Bloomsbury, who believed in the project, stewarded the contract, and shepherded it to the finish line. The finish line came into view through the meticulous attention of my copy editor and layout editor, who brought ideas to life in three-dimensional form. Form follows love, and I thank my family and friends for the steady support, encouragement, and generous space—yes, even on cruise ships and amid birthday parties—that made this labor of love possible. Now, I release it to you, dear reader.

1

Introduction

Chapter Outline

It's been a long road, bringing this book to fruition. It started as a "good idea" to invite some of my scholar-friends and colleagues to author chapters for a volume that would focus on the unique interplay between campus involvement and sense of belonging in college. I searched the *National Association of Campus Activities'* (NACA) database for recent grant winners, thinking they would make suitable contributors to this project in light of their fundable studies. You'll notice several authors are *in fact* NACA grant recipients and their chapters present key findings from those worthy investigations. But not everyone in this cast of authors is a grant recipient; rather, most are people who had *something to say* (thankfully) about sense of belonging and how campus involvement contributes to its achievement.

Sense of belonging is a fundamental basic need, a human right—just as essential as air, food, water, sleep, and shelter. That's not a political statement. It's a fact of life. My research over the last decade or so has consistently shown that belonging is a feeling (Strayhorn, 2019). It's a feeling, not an inborn trait. It's a feeling, not a biometric reading that can be altered through vaccination or medical treatment. It. Is. A. Feeling. Period. And, thus, it cannot be forced. It cannot be faked. It cannot be fabricated. It must be facilitated, nurtured, or conditioned. And that's what this book is about. It makes abundantly clear, through *research* (not hearsay) that we often create the conditions for students' sense of belonging in higher education through their active involvement in campus activities.

Belonging is defined as students' perceived social support from faculty, staff, and peers who accept and respect them for who they are, just as they are (Strayhorn, 2019). Indeed, it means loving them despite their blemishes and flaws. Belonging is explicitly linked to mattering. Mattering has four dimensions: attention, dependence, importance, and ego-extension. Attention refers to being seen in a positive light. Dependence is knowing others rely on you. Importance is feeling special and the object of one's concern. Ego-extension is having someone in your corner who celebrates your success and hurts when you fail (Schlossberg, 1989).

As I've said elsewhere, sense of belonging reflects "the individual's view of whether s/he feels included in the college community." Quite often this subjective evaluation of one's position in college takes place while considering their *elected* office in a student club, their access to campus administrators as a student leader, their accommodations as a disabled student, or their visibility as an "out" LGBTQ athlete. When student leaders interpret their time with administrators as a signal that they matter and their voices can sway decision-making, they experience a positive affective state that generally lines up with feeling a sense of belonging.

Going back, you might easily imagine the links between campus involvement, sense of belonging, and mattering for students. Mattering refers to feeling, right or wrong, that one is noticed in positive ways (attention), commands interest (importance), and contributes something beneficial to the community (dependence). It's when a student government association (SGA) officer is praised publicly for hosting a recent speaker on campus or when an intramural sports team captain feels important because others "look up" to them for camaraderie, support, and leadership.

Campus involvement is a strong predictor of sense of belonging. Astin (1999) defined involvement as the amount of physical and psychological energy that college students devote to their college experience. Campus involvement refers to ways students can participate within the college community. Involvement in college can take many forms, such as academic or social. Academic involvement includes activities like conducting research with a faculty member, engaging in study abroad, or completing internships. On the other hand, social involvement may include joining a fraternity or sorority, attending religious services, or participating in network mixers. Research consistently shows that students who are purposefully involved in college reap positive benefits that accrue to them for a lifetime (Arante et al., 2022; Doan, 2011; McAuliff et al., 2013).

I believe, more now than ever, that we've underestimated the importance of belonging in college contexts. We've chalked it up to nothing more than "skittles and rainbows," t-shirts, bumper sticks, and pep rallies. This book reminds us that fostering a deep sense of belonging for all students takes planning, thinking outside the box, and hard work, what I like to call "good work." It's good work because it aims to *do good* for those with the least. Remember this though: Belonging is not magic, never has been and never will be. But done well, belonging can produce magical results. Students who feel a strong sense of belonging engage academically. They seek help and live happier, longer lives. They marry college-educated partners and become generous alumni. They ask questions without fear of judgment and, consequently, graduate on time, just to mention a few. Feeling a sense of belonging is just that important. It's important enough for us to take action, take notice, and take it seriously.

Sense of belonging may be particularly important for students who perceive themselves as marginal to campus life, which means, by extension, that campus involvement can play a vital role for them. Being involved through clubs and organizations can provide the social bonds that one needs to be (re)connected to others who share their backgrounds, interests, and/or aspirations for the future. For instance, consider the LGBTQ student-athlete of color featured in Chapter 3 (Strayhorn & Johnson) who benefits academically and socially from supportive coaches, devoted fans, and teammates who didn't judge her based on her sexuality, but valued her humanity. Indeed, sense of belonging is a "critical aspect in retaining all students and particularly students of color" (Maestas et al., 2007, p. 238).

Academic and social involvement influences one's sense of belonging on campus. Consider the HBCU experience depicted in Chapter 4 (Burmicky & Rzucidio) highlighting the power of culturally and racially affirming spaces. Students feel safe, secure, and motivated to learn when they can let their hair down, speak slang, and show up just as they are. Motivated students seek opportunities to get involved whether it's joining a Greek letter organization, engaging in research with faculty, or making a new friend in class. Students take risks despite the dangerous consequences of rejection or refusal because the general sway of conditions is set for them to lean in, let go, and thrive.

Connecting with peers and the institution helps bolster students' sense of belonging and vice versa (Kuh et al., 2005). Belonging is "relational and, thus there's a reciprocal quality to relationships that provide a sense of belonging" (Strayhorn, 2019, p. 4). It's important to note that it depends upon interactions that are relational, not transactional. Transactional interactions tend to emphasize cost, protocol, and standards, giving short shrift to the power of connection, person-centered approaches, and issues of trust. Figure 1.1 presents a summary. To truly foster students' sense of belonging in higher education, we must prioritize relational principles.

Promoting educationally purposeful engagement with faculty, staff, peers, and the campus ecology is essential for increasing students' sense of belonging at the institution. Purposeful engagement typically refers to actively participating in various activities and initiatives on a college campus with deliberate goal(s) in mind. Chief among the consummate goals in higher education are learning, active participation in democracy, and resolving conflicts, as illustrated by several chapter authors. For example, consider the differential impacts campus involvement has on students based on their identities and where they attend school in Chapter 2 (Soria et al). Sense of belonging takes on heightened importance in certain contexts, conditions, and circumstances. Black students may feel a sense of belonging at the Black Cultural Center yet feel alienated or excluded at the school-wide ice-cream social. Disabled students, managing

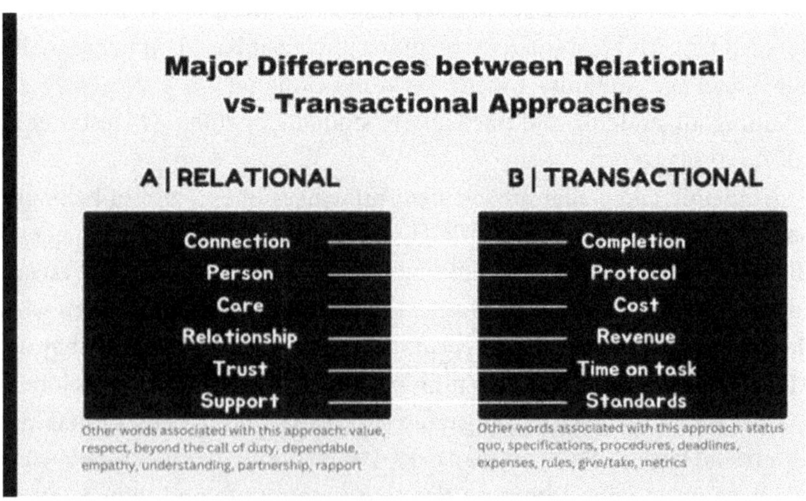

Figure 1.1 Taxonomy of relational versus transactional approaches.

mental health challenges, might feel a deep sense of belonging in the Active Minds club but feel insecure and unsafe in math class, for instance.

All in all, the chapters in this volume were recruited to sound a single alarm, calling attention to the "lived experiences" of students actively involved in campus activities. I turn to a description of the book's chapters in the next section.

Contents of the Book

The front matter provides an overview of the book, including acknowledgments, a foreword by a noted scholar on student engagement, and a preface detailing the rationale for focusing on campus involvement and sense of belonging. It establishes the book's purpose as a resource for researchers, practitioners, and policymakers aiming to understand and foster belonging through engagement in college environments.

The introductory chapter sets the foundation for the book by defining key concepts, including "sense of belonging" and "campus involvement," and explaining their significance for student success. Strayhorn reviews relevant theories, such as his framework on belonging and Astin's student involvement theory, laying out the structure of the book. He emphasizes the central thesis that active engagement in clubs and organizations is a powerful tool for promoting belonging, particularly for historically underrepresented groups.

The second chapter, "Generation Covid and the College Experience," examines the unique challenges faced by Generation Covid, the cohort of students whose college experiences were shaped by the pandemic. Authors explore how social distancing, remote learning, and economic uncertainties impacted students' sense of belonging and participation in campus activities. Drawing on qualitative and quantitative data, they highlight creative strategies that campuses used to maintain connection and engagement during unprecedented times.

"I'm More than an Athlete" by Strayhorn and Johnson investigates the intersectional experiences of Black LGBTQ+ student-athletes, exploring how their identities influence their sense of belonging on campus. Using personal narratives and survey data, the authors reveal the unique challenges faced by these students, such as navigating homophobia, gendered racism, and athletic stereotypes. The chapter concludes with actionable recommendations for athletic departments and campus administrators to better support the holistic development of Black LGBTQ+ student-athletes.

Focusing on an HBCU campus, Burmicky and Rzucidlo coauthor a chapter that critiques how social class and family legacy contribute to elitism within historically Black institutions. Authors explore how these dynamics shape students' sense of belonging, sometimes creating barriers for first-generation or economically disadvantaged students. Using rich, qualitative case studies, the chapter unpacks the tension between inclusivity and internal stratification on HBCU campuses.

Malewski and colleagues' chapter titled "Toward Beloved Communities on Campus" explores how intersectional identities, including race, gender, and sexuality, influence students' perceptions of belonging. Using the concept of "beloved community," authors argue for a rethinking of campus resources to center equity and inclusion. They provide examples of programs and initiatives that use intersectional approaches to foster meaningful engagement and a sense of community among diverse student populations.

Adding an important and somewhat unique perspective to belonging matters, Mayhew, Shaheen, and Winkler's "Centering Relationships" chapter delves into the role of religious, spiritual, and secular identities in shaping students' sense of belonging. Authors draw on survey data and in-depth interviews to explore how faith-based student organizations and interfaith initiatives foster community, particularly for marginalized religious identities. The chapter provides a nuanced discussion of how colleges can respect diverse beliefs while promoting inclusive belonging through campus involvement.

Chapter 7 titled "The Conditional Effects of Participating in a Student Organization" (by Soria, Standley, and Braun) investigates the varying impacts of student organization participation on sense of belonging, with a focus on how demographic and institutional factors shape these effects. Using a large dataset from multiple campuses, authors uncover conditional effects based on race, gender, and type of institution. They argue that student organizations are a critical pathway to belonging but must be supported through intentional, equity-focused policies.

In a bit of a break from the norm, the chapter by Thomas and Philpot juxtaposes Strayhorn's model of belonging, student involvement, and the authors' TRIFECTA framework to chart new ground on these issues at HBCUs. TRIFECTA, an acronym, stands for core components of a model that include, without limits, welcoming, holistic, open, and liberating environments. Mapping students' experiences onto the model helps illuminate the role that emancipation, liberation, and the WHOLE student experience play in facilitating students' sense of belonging through involvement in campus activities at America's Black colleges.

Chapter 9 brings Strayhorn and Johnson back together for a riveting discussion that focuses on Black college men with disabilities and how being multiply situated in society shapes their sense of belonging on- and off-campus. Using insights from a preliminary analysis of one-on-one qualitative interviews with Black disabled men, they found that race, gender, and disability play a major role in their interpretation of everyday experiences. Results from this study highlight that disabled students are very much involved, but certain aspects of campus environments disabled them from fully participating on- and off-campus. A set of recommendations for future policy, practice, and research is included.

The *Epilogue* synthesizes key themes from the book, emphasizing the importance of campus involvement as a tool for fostering belonging and promoting student success. It includes Strayhorn's reflections on the future of research and practice in this area, urging institutions to center student voices and experiences in their efforts to create inclusive and engaging campus environments.

References

Arante, R. B., Alan, F. A. O., & Beray, M. J. M. (2022). Exploratory analysis of students' awareness and involvement in campus organizations: Its influence on their leadership skills. *Science International Lahore*, *34*(2), 111–115.

Astin, A. W. (1999). Student involvement: A developmental theory for higher education. Journal of College Student Development, 40(5), 518–529.

Doan, J. (2011). The impact of campus climate and student involvement on students of color. *The Vermont Connection*, *32*(1), 4.

Kuh, G. D., Kinzie, J., Schuh, J. H., Whitt, E. J., & Associates. (2005). Student success in college: Creating conditions that matter. Jossey-Bass.

Maestas, R., Vaquera, G. S., & Zehr, L. M. (2007). Factors impacting sense of belonging at a Hispanic-serving institution. Journal of Hispanic Higher Education, 6(3), 237–256.

McAuliff, K. E., Williams, S. M., & Ferrari, J. R. (2013). Social justice and the university community: Does campus involvement make a difference?. *Journal of Prevention & Intervention in the Community, 41*(4), 244–254.

Schlossberg, N. K. (1989). Marginality and mattering: Key issues in building community. New directions for student services.

Strayhorn, T. L. (2019). College students' sense of belonging: A key to educational success for all students (2nd ed.). Routledge.

2

Generation Covid and the College Experience

Exploring the Reverberations of 2020 on Young People's Transition and Engagement

Gabriel Velez, Jody Jessup-Anger, Max Herteen, and Sam Nemanich

---

Chapter Outline

Introduction

In early 2020, Covid-19 began to spread in the United States, causing a major disruption of everyday life for everyone, including millions of young people. Schools were closed or moved online, extracurricular activities were canceled, and mandated quarantine meant limited opportunities to engage with peers in person. Covid-related impacts on young people have been extensive: forced disconnection, social isolation, loss of support systems, disrupted routines, academic gaps, and more (e.g., Hussong et al., 2021).

Although the pandemic has shifted and become normalized as time has passed, the disruptions experienced by adolescents early on shaped their development and thus will likely shape their transitions to and experiences during college. Youth who were in high school in 2020 are now attending postsecondary institutions, carrying with them the reverberations of pandemic-impacted time on their social, academic, and personal development. With this in mind, our study asked, how did the experience of the early pandemic resonate with students as they transitioned to college? Specifically, we investigated how it influenced their ability to connect with others and their engagement on campus.

Literature Review

Adolescence and emerging adulthood are formative times in the life course. Embedded within social contexts and markers such as high school graduation, young people are establishing more lasting identities, building social connections, and developing visions of their futures, which include postsecondary experiences and trajectories (Arnett, 2015). In these psychosocial processes, they draw heavily on experiences with and perceptions of friends, family, and peers in school (Eccles & Roeser, 2011).

Social, personal, and academic experiences in high school can set the stage for students' transition to college. For instance, decades of research suggest that high school academic preparation is a strong predictor of college persistence toward graduation and eases the transition to college (e.g., Adelman, 1999; Goldrick-Rab et al., 2007; Stage & Hossler, 2000). Co-curricular and social connections also drive the college transition experience and enrich student learning outcomes (Astin, 1993). Moreover, co-curricular participation in high school often creates habits of mind that lay a solid foundation for continued involvement in college (Renn & Reason, 2013). Such a foundation helps ease the transition to college and potentially sets students up for long-term college success.

Previous researchers have found that college students' "engagement in educationally purposeful activities is a key component to their success" (Manning et al., 2014, p. 18). Productive activities include participating in research with faculty, learning communities, internships, and service learning (AACU, 2007), to name a few. All too often, students self-select into these experiences based, in part, on their high school engagement (Berk & Goebel, 1987; Kuh, 2008).

Peers play an instrumental role in how students navigate college and whether they develop interpersonal skills, resolve self-esteem, and feel supported (Astin, 1993; McCabe, 2016). Related to students' peer relationships is their sense of belonging, which Strayhorn (2019) defines as "students' perceived social support on campus, a feeling or sensation of connectedness, the experience of mattering or feeling cared about, accepted, respected, valued by, and important to the group (e.g., campus community) or others on campus (e.g., faculty, peers)" (p. 3). Peers can be a major source of support, connectedness, and mattering, but other relationships also affect students' sense of belonging. As might be expected, students report that having relationships with faculty and staff helps them feel connected to their academics. Developing deeper interactions with faculty, those defined as connected to meaning and value, can help students to find a greater sense of community on campus (Sriram et al., 2020).

Since Covid-19 forced disconnection and strict physical distancing from faculty and peers, it seems reasonable to assume that dimensions of belonging also shifted. For example, high school juniors and seniors experienced lockdowns during a time typically marked by significant academic and social milestones such as prom, standardized tests, and college tours. Consequently, many missed co-curricular activities and were left to quickly adapt to higher-level coursework and new social interactions as they transitioned to college.

Research suggests the social isolation caused by pandemic-related shutdowns and quarantine measures broadly impacted adolescent well-being. Lockdown and physical distancing measures significantly reduced adolescents' opportunities for socializing (Branje & Morris, 2021). Adolescents reported reduced affiliation with friends and structured social groups, as well as lower levels of support from friends. Social isolation contributed to negative mental health outcomes, which has led to record-setting increases in adolescent anxiety, depression, and loneliness during the pandemic (Rogers et al., 2021; Samji et al., 2021, Velez et al., 2022; Zolopa et al., 2022).

Young people were also disconnected from their academic lives. Studies have found that adolescent school bonding through school clubs and activities decreased during the pandemic (Maiya et al., 2021), as well as steep drops in their academic well-being, lower school engagement, and higher burnout during the pandemic (Salmela-Aro et al., 2021). In an investigation of challenges adolescents experienced early in the pandemic, Scott and colleagues (2021) reported that 24 percent of participants had academic struggles due to negative experiences with online learning, decreased focus, and difficulties with time management. Respondents also noted that the loss of normal activities such as entertainment and scheduled events contributed to lower rates of academic success and worsened mental health.

We aimed to build on this literature demonstrating the impact of 2020 on adolescents by exploring how these experiences informed young people's transition to college. This research is important to better understand how these cohorts may be engaging with their college campuses, as well as challenges to their sense of belonging and academic success.

The Study

Research Design

Our study employed a mixed-methods approach to understanding connections between Covid-19 experiences and various measures of well-being, identity, future thinking, and perceptions of college experience.

We surveyed a group of first-time, first-year college students in the fall of 2021 to explore relationships between these quantitative measures, and then interviewed a separate group of students twice over the course of their freshman year via Microsoft Teams. All procedures were approved by the researchers' institutional review board (IRB).

Sample

Both samples came from the same mid-sized, private, urban Midwestern university. The survey was sent to a randomly sampled third sample of the first-year class in the first three weeks of the semester. The final sample (N = 109, 18 percent response rate) mirrored institutional demographics for the first-year class: 60.5 percent identified as white, 16 percent Latinx, 9 percent Black, and around a quarter (23 percent) had received free/reduced school lunch in high school.

Interview invitations were sent to all incoming students as part of institutional emails. To encourage diverse representation among the sample, specific emails were sent to prospective participants via programs serving large numbers of first-generation students and students of color. Interview participants were randomly selected from the list of those who expressed interest, with a goal of scheduling 40 participants. Ultimately, we interviewed 36 participants whose demographics were similar to the survey group: 50 percent identified as white, 25 percent as Latinx, 6 percent as Black, and 25 percent indicated that they had received free/reduced school lunch. Interview participants came from all 7 of the university's colleges, with the most from Health Sciences (n = 8) and Arts and Sciences (n = 9).

Measures

The survey took approximately fifteen minutes and included measures of wellness, campus experiences, future thinking, Covid-19 experiences, and demographics. Wellness was measured using the *General Anxiety Disorder-7 Scale* (Spitzer et al., 2006) and the *Patient Health Questionnaire-9* (Kroenke et al., 2001). Campus experiences were measured with an adaptation of items from the *First-Time Freshman Survey* (Wawrzynski & Jessup-Anger, 2010), sense of belonging was a 3-item scale (Haussman et al., 2007). Covid-19 experiences were measured with the *-19 Exposure and Family Impact Survey* Adolescent and Young Adult Version (CEFIS-AYA; Schwartz et al., 2022). The measure has three parts focusing on exposure (i.e., 28 dichotomous items), impact (i.e., 15 four-point Likert items and 1 item with a 10-point distress scale with 1 being no distress and 10 being extremely distressed), an open-ended response about experiences, and has been validated with large samples of young adults in the United States (Schwartz et al., 2022).

The interview protocol was developed by the research team to explore students' experiences with Covid-19, lasting impacts of these experiences, physical and mental health, and thinking about college and the future. Sample questions included: Have you made any changes in how you approach your schooling or learning during the Covid-19 pandemic? What were some supports that helped you over the last year and a half? Other questions gauged future and college thinking such as: Has the pandemic changed your thinking about your future at all? What are you looking forward to the most about your first year at college? For more information about the interview protocol, contact the authors.

Positionality

As researchers, we come from diverse disciplines and work as faculty or graduate students at the institution where the study was conducted. Three of us had conducted previous research on the pandemic's impact on children and youth. With these varied backgrounds, our goal was to develop a holistic approach to studying how young people were thinking about and experienced the transition to college given their Covid-19 experiences. For example, we included measures on physical and mental well-being, future thinking, identity, and belonging, and our research design and data analysis were informed by literature from health science, psychology, and higher education studies. Our project was also structured to provide actionable information to staff on campus providing support to these students. Therefore, we collaborated with various campus offices during recruitment and presented preliminary findings in meetings with administrators and with student affairs professionals in various offices to hear their reactions and solicit feedback.

Trustworthiness

Throughout the data collection and analysis process, we strove to incorporate internal and external feedback. First, the primary researchers are all early- to mid-career academics, so we intentionally involved our three graduate research assistants in developing protocol questions and analyzing interview data. We also ensured that participants did not previously know the researcher assigned to interview them to minimize complications from previous relationships between faculty and students. Finally, we met throughout the interview periods to reflect on how we thought our roles might have been influencing participants' responses.

Since this research also aimed to support work on campus, we drew on feedback external to the research team to situate our analyses within a broader context. Specifically, in our conversations with administrators and student affairs professionals on campus, we solicited feedback about the themes and took notes on their reactions and responses. These insights were considered by our research team as part of the final analyses.

Data Analysis

Survey data were extracted from Qualtrics and exported for analysis using statistical software. Descriptive statistics were calculated, and linear regression analysis was used to examine the relationship between sense of belonging and overall distress from the Covid-19 pandemic, accounting for covariates of race, ethnicity, gender, and free/reduced lunch status.

Interview transcriptions were produced by Otter.ai software and then read over by the research team to ensure quality and understanding. Then, two researchers read all transcripts thoroughly and conducted a first-wave coding for the different sections. Next, they followed a collaborative inductive coding process focused on parts related to specific research questions (Braun & Clarke, 2022). This began with a first round random sample (20 percent) to discuss discrepancies and ensure reliability. Once all sections related to research questions were coded, the researchers met to discuss emerging themes, return to the data, and adjust findings.

Key Findings

Quantitative

Survey results indicated that the pandemic had a detrimental effect on students' physical health, with even worse impacts on mental health and relationships (see Table 2.1). The vast majority noted that Covid-19 disrupted their education (94.7 percent) and made them miss an important family event (83.2 percent) or milestone (e.g., high school graduation, prom; 82.3 percent). Overall, students expressed mild distress in relation to the pandemic ($M = 5.47$, $SD = 1.91$). Close to 3 out of 4 students said their anxiety (72.4 percent), loneliness (73.8 percent), and mood (71.6 percent) were all worsened by the pandemic. Almost a third (29 percent) were at risk for depression and anxiety disorders. This rate was higher for students of color (37.8 percent).

Interestingly, these students did not demonstrate disengagement from campus as they started their college experiences. Over 70 percent of students responded that they agree (somewhat or strongly) with all three of the belonging items. Psychological indicators of campus engagement were also high; 66.7 percent were likely to take on a leadership position on or off-campus, and 67.5 percent were likely to join a campus, departmental, or hall organization.[1] There were stark differences by race/ethnicity and first-generation status. For example, while almost a third of the overall sample said they felt a sense of belonging, only 58.5 percent of students of

Table 2.1 *Sense of Belonging Measure*

Variable	Number of students who agreed or strongly agreed	Percentage of respondents
I feel a sense of belonging to my institution	83	72.8
I am happy to be at my institution	92	90.7
I see myself as part of my institution's community	82	71.9

[1]In this chapter, "likely" refers to both "somewhat" and "very likely" ratings.

Table 2.2 *Regression Results for Comparing Covid Distress and Sense of Belonging*

Effect	Estimate	SE	*p*
Intercept	1.61	16.34	
Covid Distress	−0.192	0.16	0.23
Gender	−0.042	0.59	0.94
Race	−2.385	0.73	<0.01
Ethnicity	1.74	1.06	0.10
Free Lunch Status	−0.788	0.76	0.30

color and 46.1 percent of first-generation students agreed (somewhat or strongly).

We also explored relationships between sense of belonging and distress, as measured by the CEFIS. Linear regression results were statistically non-significant (see Table 2.2), failing to show a relationship between sense of belonging and stress after accounting for covariates of race, ethnicity, and free/reduced lunch status. Race was a significant covariate consistent with descriptive results: non-white students of color experienced lower levels of belonging compared to white students.

Qualitative

In the interviews, participants detailed high levels of stress and disruption across various aspects of their life during the pandemic. Still, their takeaways from these experiences as they began college were not always negative. While many talked about being worried about the academic transition, others detailed how they learned coping strategies and grew in positive ways that they carried with them into college. On the whole, they expressed excitement as they looked forward to (re)engaging socially with peers and professors.

Many participants described mental health challenges related to the pandemic and highlighted being worried about the continuing uncertainty of Covid-19 as they transitioned to college. They described struggles with motivation, stress, and isolation during remote schooling and quarantines. They missed friends, were upset about losing out on celebratory experiences in high school like graduation and prom, and many were either disengaged or overwhelmed by academic expectations. At the same time, they also described growing self-awareness, including about mental health needs and effective coping strategies. One participant said, "This pandemic taught me that time is of the essence. Anything can change in a heartbeat, so I see just doing like Nike: Just do it. And that's with my schoolwork and that's in relationships with my friends or family. That's all my future job." Another noted that it supported his growing independence: "It helped me kind of develop ways to remain fit on my own, ways to study effectively on my own, to kind of continue my learning on my own."

Framing academic experiences and personal growth in such ways also played into how they described their thinking about the transition to college. Participants perceived remote schooling as difficult, unpleasant, and challenging. Many expressed worries about renewed social distancing restrictions because of difficult experiences they had with these policies and remote schooling during their final high school years.

Whereas some students found online learning in high school difficult, others perceived it as easier than normal. For example, one shared that classes were like "cake. I slept through every class and I finished with straight A's. It was simple." In general, academic experiences during the pandemic left such students feeling unprepared for college. One said, "I am going to get a rude awakening when I come to college. I know that for a fact. I am a very hardworking person . . . It's just when it comes to school, I'm just not going to be prepared." Another was more specific, noting that their chemistry and algebra classes were particularly hard: "When I went to do an assignment to see how much I knew, I didn't know anything. And that was all of the things that I was supposed to learn last year during my senior year, so I was pretty lost."

Others felt more confident because of new strategies they developed and a related sense of independence. These students—a minority—described both attitudinal and practical skills (e.g., time management) that would help them in college. One noted that taking ownership of his learning helped to "kind of develop an enjoyment for learning things. I've always enjoyed learning things outside of school, and I was just able to adapt it to my current circumstances." Another described having to become more organized:

> Because a lot of things have been on my own time. Like teachers being like, okay, here's an assignment, log on for class and have it done before tomorrow . . . I became really good at just like getting things done with so

> that I could have a free time. I think even like mentally that's really helped me—picking up how to create a schedule and stick to it.

Beyond academics, participants described feeling excited and ready for college, particularly about being back in person. They expressed some concerns about classes having to go virtual, but were very much looking forward to meeting new people and having personal interactions with their professors. Some noted feeling good because unlike their senior year in high school and the first year at college for the previous cohort, they would be able to have a more typical experience: "It's definitely one of those things where you feel a little bit more grateful to be at college, especially in person because not everybody had those experiences last year."

Discussion

Although the students in this study transitioned to college in the fall of 2021, they carried experiences from the early part of the pandemic with them that affected their in-college experiences in myriad ways. Survey data demonstrated that this cohort experienced high rates of disruption across various domains of their life. Interview analyses, on the other hand, provided insights into how they experienced these disruptions and challenges, including in their academics, socializing, and personal wellness. Qualitative data further revealed that impacts lingered with them as they transitioned to college. In their academics, many worried about not being prepared, gaps in their learning, and poor study habits that developed during the previous two years. Socially, they described missing out on key markers and connections during their high school years, though few explicitly said they felt socially unprepared for college. Existing research highlights that these students were right to worry, as having a less rigorous high school experience could have implications for their college transition (Adelman, 1999; Astin & Osguera, 2004; Goldrick-Rab et al., 2007). Furthermore, these findings are in line with other work that demonstrated significant challenges to learning, lowered motivation for schoolwork, and sorrow about isolation and missed milestones (e.g., Branje & Morris, 2021; Scott et al., 2021; Velez et al., 2022).

At the same time, our participants demonstrated lasting positive takeaways. Quantitative data showed that, like students who attended college prior to the pandemic (Wawrzynski & Jessup-Anger, 2010), they had intentions to engage on campus and felt a strong sense of belonging on campus early on. Survey results were bolstered by the qualitative findings, in which participants described being excited to be back in person and were looking forward to the possibility of a more typical college experience after the disruptions of the previous few years.

Importantly, and also aligned with previous research (Strayhorn, 2019), sense of belonging was significantly lowered for the survey respondents who were Black and Latino/a or first-generation. It is important to note the study institution is a predominantly white institution, though it has been making strides toward increasing compositional diversity and has numerous diversity initiatives. Black, Latino/a, and/or first-generation students already may face challenges and obstacles systemically and socially in achieving a sense of belonging on campus (e.g., Strayhorn, 2019; Velez & Jessup-Anger, 2022). Added to this dynamic is the fact that Covid-19 and its disruptions were more acute in low-income and communities of color (e.g., Fortuna et al., 2020). These unequal impacts influenced students' experiences on their college campuses by adding further stressors (Reyes-Portillo et al., 2022).

Mental health and wellness have been a growing concern on college campuses. Our participants' responses reflect a large body of evidence that adolescents and college students were deeply emotionally impacted by the early part of the pandemic (e.g., Halliburton et al., 2021; Zolopa et al., 2022). Still, interviewees also described the ways that they had developed coping strategies or learned about themselves from struggles during the pandemic. Such a perspective does not negate the depth of the challenge they faced or the fact that they may face mental health concerns, but suggests there may be space to understand and strengthen their resilience (e.g., Luthar et al., 2021).

In relation to their social expectations, these participants generally described being excited to be on campus and looked forward to engaging with others. Nevertheless, there may be disconnects between this and how they are actually able to engage socially. The social isolation during the early pandemic deeply disrupted usual supports and contexts for social development that are critical in adolescence. Although for some young people this may have been supportive in creating new identities, for others it deeply impacted normative developmental processes. Our interviewees' responses then may reflect what they were excited about as they went to college (i.e., a return to "normal"), but they may not have been aware of the challenges they would face due to the impacts of the previous years on their social development. Moreover, postsecondary institutions were still recovering from the pandemic as these students entered college, meaning there were still social distancing mandates in classrooms and events, limits on the number of students at events, and reduced staff capacity.

Recommendations and Conclusion

An overall implication from this research is to move beyond negatively deterministic frameworks for thinking about how the Covid-19 pandemic may be affecting young people's connection and engagement as they transition to college. The challenges and reverberations are real. Still, there is the value in engaging with how young people are thinking about their Covid-19 experiences and the lasting social, academic, and personal impacts on them. Quantitative measures provide insight, but do not get at what these experiences mean to young people and what they are carrying with them as they embark on their postsecondary journeys. Engaging with this thinking can provide college personnel with important information and a point of intervention. Creating meaning and purpose from struggle is a key facet of building resilience and handling trauma. There is evidence that this is true for young people in relation to the pandemic (Booker et al., 2022), and so colleges could provide concrete opportunities to encourage this among their students.

These findings also highlight gaps and challenges that young people may need extra support in managing. While there has been widespread concern about academics and mental health due to the pandemic, there has been less focus on students processing. Our participants discussed worries about being ready for their classes in college, which could impact their ability to spend time engaging on campus or with peers or their wellness. Therefore, another important implication is that colleges should shape social and academic supports they provide in relation to how students are describing their needs. This requires intentional engagement with student voice and reconsidering programs and processes to engage students that have worked in the past.

In addition, findings highlight particular needs for students of color in relation to their sense of belonging (or lack thereof). For all students, the pandemic may have disrupted the sense of connection and mattering in relation to their educational institutions. For students of color and other marginalized students, this disruption might be particularly problematic because meaningful connections from high school are often carried with them as they transition to college. Without those steady connections, these students may feel particularly unmoored as they enter the college environment. Student affairs professionals and other university personnel should be particularly attentive to these increased challenges by ensuring students of color get connected early in their collegiate experience. Finally, it is important to contextualize this study. We focused on one school and with one cohort as they transitioned to college. Research should expand to consider these young people's trajectories through their postsecondary experiences, as well as including future cohorts and more diverse samples.

Overall, this chapter demonstrates value in exploring the way a sample of students think about and experience the transition to college in relation to experiences from early in the Covid-19 pandemic (see Table 2.3 for summary of takeaways). Using a mixed-methods approach, we investigated this question for one cohort of students entering college in the fall of 2021. These students were clearly deeply impacted by the pandemic and reported significant challenges to academic and mental well-being, but also

Table 2.3 *Summary of Takeaways*

Number	Summary
1	Quantitative measures indicated disruption, distress, and mental health challenges due to the pandemic, but also robust sense of belonging and intent to engage on campus.
2	In interviews a separate sample of participants similarly described stress and mental health concerns during the early part of the pandemic.
3	Many of the interviewees, however, also described experiencing personal and academic growth from these challenges, as well as excitement for a "normal" college experience following restrictions and social distancing during the early part of the pandemic.
4	Overall, the findings indicate that static measures of negative experiences related to the pandemic may hide other areas of development, growth, and strength that will serve young people as they transition to college.

demonstrated resilience and coping. It is noteworthy that their sense of belonging was high, which may be tied into the ways they made meaning out of the challenges of the early pandemic and were looking forward to more typical college experiences. Still, our data indicated divergent experiences for Black, Latino/a, and/or first-generation students, building on a wealth of research from before the pandemic and evidence that the communities these students were most likely from experienced disproportionate impacts from Covid-19. Looking to the future, it is critical that research and programming seeking to bolster belonging and involvement considers these complexities in how students made meaning from the pandemic and carry forth the impacts of 2020 and 2021 with them as they transition to college.

References

Adelman, C. (1999). *Answers in the tool box: Academic intensity, attendance patterns, and bachelor's degree attainment.* U.S. Department of Education. https://www2.ed.gov/rschstat/research/pubs/toolboxrevisit/toolbox.pdf

Arnett, J. J. (2015). Identity development from adolescence to emerging adulthood: What we know and (especially) don't know. In K. C. McLean & M. Syed (Eds.), *The Oxford handbook of identity development* (pp. 53–64). Oxford University Press.

Association of American Colleges and Universities [AACU]. (2007). *College learning and the new global century.* Author.

Astin, A.W. (1993). *What matters in college? Four critical years revisited.* Jossey-Bass.

Astin, A. W., & Osguera, L. (2004). The declining "equity" of higher education. *Review of Higher Education, 27*(3), 321–341. https://doi.org/10.1353/rhe.2004.0001

Berk, L. E., & Goebel, B. L. (1987). Patterns of extracurricular participation from high school to college. *American Journal of Education, 95*(3), 468–485.

Booker, J. A., Ell, M., Fivush, R., Greenhoot, A. F., McLean, K. C., Wainryb, C., & Pasupathi, M. (2022). Early impacts of college, interrupted: considering first-year students' narratives about covid and reports of adjustment during college shutdowns. *Psychological Science, 33*(11), 1928–1946. https://doi.org/10.1177/09567976221108941

Branje, S., & Morris, A. S. (2021). The impact of the Covid-19 pandemic on adolescent emotional, social, and academic adjustment. *Journal of Research on Adolescence, 31*(3), 486–499.

Braun, V., & Clarke, V. (2022). Conceptual and design thinking for thematic analysis. *Qualitative Psychology, 9*(1), 3–26. https://doi.org/10.1037/qup0000196

Eccles, J. S., & Roeser, R. W. (2011). Schools as developmental contexts during adolescence. *Journal of Research on Adolescence, 21*(1), 225–241.

Fortuna, L. R., Tolou-Shams, M., Robles-Ramamurthy, B., & Porche, M. V. (2020). Inequity and the disproportionate impact of Covid-19 on communities of color in the United States: The need for a trauma-informed social justice response. *Psychological Trauma: Theory, Research, Practice, and Policy, 12*(5), 443.

Goldrick-Rab, S., Carter, D. F., & Winkle Wagner, R. (2007). What higher education has to say about the transition to college. *Teachers College Record, 109*, 2444–2481.

Halliburton, A. E., Hill, M. B., Dawson, B. L., Hightower, J. M., & Rueden, H. (2021). Increased stress, declining mental health: Emerging adults' experiences in college during Covid-19. *Emerging Adulthood, 9*(5), 433–448. https://doi.org/10.1177/21676968211025348

Haussman, L. R. M., Schofield, J. W., & Woods, R. L. (2007). Sense of belonging as a predictor of intentions to persist among African American and white first-year college students. *Research in Higher Education, 48*, 803–839.

Hussong, A. M., Benner, A. D., Erdem, G., Lansford, J. E., Makila, L. M., & Petrie, R. C. (2021). Adolescence amid a pandemic: Short and long-term implications. *Journal of Research on Adolescence, 31*(3), 820–835. https://doi.org/10.1111/jora.12671

Kroenke, K., Spitzer, R. L., & Williams, J. B. (2001). The PHQ-9: Validity of a brief depression severity measure. *Journal of General Internal Medicine, 16*(9), 606–613.

Kuh, G. D. (2008). *High-impact educational practices: What they are, who has access to them, and why they matter*. Association of American Colleges & Universities.

Luthar, S. S., Pao, L. S., & Kumar, N. L. (2021). Covid-19 and resilience in schools: Implications for practice and policy. *Social Policy Report, 34*(3), 1–65.

Maiya, S., Dotterer, A. M., & Whiteman, S. D. (2021). Longitudinal changes in adolescents' school bonding during the Covid-19 pandemic:

Individual, parenting, and family correlates. *Journal of Research on Adolescence, 31*(3), 808–819.

Manning, K., Kinzie, J., & Schuh, J. H. (2014). *One size does not fit all: Traditional and innovative models of student affairs practice.* Routledge.

McCabe, J. M. (2016). *Connecting in college: How friendship networks matter for academic and social success.* University of Chicago Press.

Reyes-Portillo, J. A., Masia Warner, C., Kline, E. A., Bixter, M. T., Chu, B. C., Miranda, R., Nadeem, E., Nickerson, A., Ortin Peralta, A., & Reigada, L. (2022). The psychological, academic, and economic impact of Covid-19 on college students in the epicenter of the pandemic. *Emerging Adulthood, 10*(2), 473–490.

Renn, K. R., & Reason, R. D. (2013). *College students in the United States: Characteristics, experiences, and outcomes.* Jossey-Bass.

Rogers, A. A., Ha, T., & Ockey, S. (2021). Adolescents' perceived socio-emotional impact of Covid-19 and implications for mental health: Results from a U.S.-Based mixed-methods study. *Journal of Adolescent Health, 68*(1), 43–52.

Salmela-Aro, K., Upadyaya, K., Vinni-Laakso, J., & Hietajärvi, L. (2021). Adolescents' longitudinal school engagement and burnout before and during Covid-19—The role of socio-emotional skills. *Journal of Research on Adolescence, 31*(3), 796–807.

Samji, H., Wu, J., Ladak, A., Vossen, C., Stewart, E., Dove, N., Long, D., & Snell, G. (2021). Mental health impacts of the Covid-19 pandemic on children and youth–a systematic review. *Child and Adolescent Mental Health, 27*(2), 173–189. https://doi.org/10.1111/camh.12501

Schwartz, L. A., Lewis, A. M., Alderfer, M. A., Vega, G., Barakat, L. P., King-Dowling, S., . . . Kazak, A. (2022). Covid-19 exposure and family impact scales for adolescents and young adults. *Journal of Pediatric Psychology, 47*(6), 631–640.

Scott, S. R., Rivera, K. M., Rushing, E., Manczak, E. M., Rozek, C. S., & Doom, J. R. (2021). "I hate this": A qualitative analysis of adolescents' self-reported challenges during the Covid-19 pandemic. *Journal of Adolescent Health, 68*(2), 262–269.

Spitzer, R. L., Kroenke, K., Williams, J. B., & Löwe, B. (2006). A brief measure for assessing generalized anxiety disorder: The GAD-7. *Archives of Internal Medicine, 166*(10), 1092–1097.

Sriram, R., Weintraub, S. D., Murray, J. L. Cheatle, J., Haynes, C., & Marquart, C. P. (2020). The influence of social, academic, and deeper life interactions on psychological sense of community in college students. *Journal of College Student Development, 61*(5), 593–605.

Stage, F. K. & Hossler, D. (2000). Where is the student? Linking student behaviors, college choice, and college persistence. In J. Braxton (Ed.), *Reworking the student departure puzzle* (pp. 170–195). Vanderbilt University Press.

Strayhorn, T. L. (2019). *College students' sense of belonging: A key to educational success for all students*. Routledge.

Velez, G., Hahn, M., & Troyer, B. (2022). Making meaning of Covid-19: US adolescent experiences and development amid the pandemic. *Translational Issues in Psychological Science*, *8*(2), 269–281.

Velez, G., & Jessup-Anger, J. E. (2022). Messaging and action around race and inclusion at a predominantly white institution: Perceived dissonance of black, indigenous, and people of color students. *Emerging Adulthood*, *10*(4), 852–858.

Wawrzynski, M. R., & Jessup-Anger, J. E. (2010). From expectations to experiences: Using a structural typology to understand first-year student outcomes in academically based living-learning environments. *Journal of College Student Development*, *51*, 201–217.

Zolopa, C., Burack, J. A., O'Connor, R. M., Corran, C., Lai, J., Bomfim, E., DeGrace, S., Dumont, J., Larney, S., & Wendt, D. C. (2022). Changes in youth mental health, psychological wellbeing, and substance use during the Covid-19 pandemic: A rapid review. *Adolescent Research Review*, *7*, 1–17.

3

"I'm More Than an Athlete"

Exploring Sense of Belonging in College for Black LGBTQ+ Student-Athletes

Terrell L. Strayhorn and J'Quen O. Johnson

Chapter Outline

Introduction | Our Argument

It was a cold, rainy Thursday evening when Chayla (pronounced "Shay-luh"), a sophomore, walked into the campus cultural center to participate in a group interview study focused on the experiences of college students of color at predominantly white institutions (PWIs). The dimly lit conference room filled with the soft sound of jazz music, an intentional strategy used by the lead author's research team to welcome students, gain rapport, ease their mind, and offer solace from the storm brewing outside. We handed out snacks, got signatures on the *Informed Consent* form, and then geared up for the group interview to begin.

Shortly after the interview started, Chayla shared: "As a Black lesbian basketball player at a major D1 [NCAA Division 1] school who stands over 6-feet tall, I feel like I might have a unique kinda experience . . . ." Head nods and sounds from her peers in the room signaled full agreement with the observation. Chayla went on to talk about how she feels enormous pressure to "hold it all together," to "keep it all in," referring to her sexuality, same-sex attractions, and steady relationship with a sorority woman (non-athlete) who attends a nearby historically Black college/university (HBCU). Through examples and anecdotes, she whispers, at times through tears, about coaches and fans who frequently celebrated her athletic skills and talents, but denied, ignored, or criticized her sexual orientation and relationship stories. "You too pretty [*sic*] and smart to be a lesbian . . . or you're such a great player, don't let this thing ruin your career," both illustrative quotes reflect the hurtful comments that Chayla endured about her sexuality from alleged "well-intended caring adults."

Interestingly, her voice brightened and picked up speed at one point. She shared: "But that's just my experience in sports as a Black gay woman who plays ball . . . it's outside of the irongrid [referring to sports] that I've really found *my squad* [emphasis added]." With energy and obvious excitement, she talked at length about "Shades," a registered student organization for LGBTQ+ students of color, where she "held an important role as co-program chair." Black Scholars International ([BSI] a pseudonym), a campus club for Black international students that has "the best food fest . . . period" in her opinion (laughing). And "Music to the Masses," a service-learning project sponsored by her school that works to bring music (especially jazz) to low-income and disenfranchised communities. "The people who I've met through Shades, BSI, and M2M [Music to the Masses] . . . they my peeps [*sic*], they know the *real me* and they accept me for who I am, truly, no lie. Man, I wish it was like that in the department [referring to Athletics]. . .'cuz I know I play there, but it never feels like home, you know, I'm more than an athlete." Again, the nods, smiles, and high-fives from Black peers in the room seemed to affirm that yes, indeed, her story resonated with many others.

Little did Chayla know that her story that gloomy evening would illuminate the pages of our chapter-length exploration into the intricate world of Black LGBTQ+ college student-athletes' sense of belonging many years later. With each word spoken and each experience shared, Chayla unknowingly guided us through the uncharted terrain of acceptance, connections, mattering, and other key elements that would later give rise to a sense of belonging theory (Strayhorn, 2019). As Chayla's story intertwined with those of her peers, a powerful narrative emerged–one that transcends the boundaries of race, the "closet" of sexuality, and the "irongrid" of athletics, reaching deeper into the intersectional lives of college students who are at once both *Black and LGBTQ+ and student-athletes and so much more*. We know that identities matter, but recognize a need for exploring and understanding if and how intersecting identities play out in campus involvement experiences for this specific student population.

Problem Statement

Diverse identities uniquely shape LGBTQ+[1] students' experiences in college (Ottenritter, 2012) and it seems reasonable to presume the same holds true in intercollegiate athletics. Consider, for example, the number of women who compete in college sports today, roughly 226,000 according to the NCAA. This represents a 5 percent increase from 2020–

[1]We intentionally use different acronyms over the course of this chapter to acknowledge the term's evolution over time as society gains more understanding of sex, gender, and sexual orientations, and more groups are intentionally included. Thus, LGBTQIA2S+ refers to lesbian, gay, bisexual, trans, queer/questioning, intersex, asexual, two-spirit, and "+" representing members of the community whose identity is not yet included or words cannot yet fully describe.

21, one of the largest shifts for women in the last twenty years. There are also rising numbers of college student-athletes[2] with disabilities, although national estimates of this kind are largely unknown and not documented (Stokowski & O'Donnell, 2022). And despite significant steps taken toward greater inclusion of lesbian, gay, bisexual, transgender, and queer (LGBTQ+) professional athletes (King, 2017) and college student-athletes in competitive environments, heterosexist and homophobic attitudes run rampant and permeate much of the college sports world (Rankin, 2012).

Nowhere is this more evident than among Black LGBTQ+ students *and* student-athletes who continue to face ongoing racial discrimination and homophobia (even violence) in athletics, higher education, and broader society (Brody et al., 2022). From racial- and sexual-identity based discrimination in team selection to racialized stereotypes that cast them as athletes–not academics–Black LGBTQ+ student-athletes' lived experiences underscore the complex ways in which race, gender, and sexual orientation affect one's perceptions of college and campus life.

Challenges faced by Black LGBTQ+ student-athletes have been examined in prior studies, which we'll review later in the chapter. Black LGBTQ+ students, some even being student-athletes, for instance, report hearing homophobic and racist slurs like "fag," "nigga," or "dyke" in campus spaces (e.g., locker rooms), among peers, in online dating apps, and even short message service (SMS) group chats (Havey, 2021). Other studies have shown that some Black LGBTQ+ athletes have experienced physical violence from teammates and fans (Turk et al., 2019), underscoring the critical importance of safety and security issues for college students generally and student-athletes specifically. Safety and security are also basic building blocks of student belonging according to theory (Strayhorn, 2019).

Beyond teammates, there's empirical evidence of harassment, threats, and hostility from coaches and staff toward LGBTQ+ student-athletes of color, such as Black lesbian basketball players (Newhall & Buzuvis, 2008). Consequently, some Black LGBTQ+ student-athletes are hesitant to disclose their sexual orientation to others within athletic departments.

---

[2]We refer to student-athletes as students who are members of a team sponsored by the institution's athletics department, which may not include students who participate in intramural, community, and/or recreational sports.

Others either deny, suppress, or ignore their same-sex feelings, which can lead to a range of mental health issues such as anxiety, depression, self-hatred, and suicidal ideation (e.g., Anderson et al., 2023). Data clearly indicate that all of these can compromise athletic and academic performance, as measured by class attendance, grades, and retention (Cunningham, 2015; Wolf-Wendel et al., 2008).

Other significant factors facilitate the academic- and athletic success of Black student-athletes in collegiate sports such as sense of belonging (Cooper & Newton, 2021; Carter-Francique, 2018), a major variable that's highly correlated with educational success (Strayhorn, 2019). Sense of belonging refers to feelings of connectedness or beliefs about one's importance to the campus community and other campus members such as faculty, staff, and peers. For instance, Gaston Gayles et al. (2018) analyzed survey data from 7,703 Division I student-athletes at over 630 institutions. They found significant differences in overall sense of belonging between student-athletes of color and their white counterparts, with students of color reporting lower belonging scores on average. Similar results were found between revenue- and non-revenue generating sports. Academic factors that matter include grades, year in school, and social involvement in various activities such as internships, hanging out with peers, or speaking with a professor outside of class, to name a few.

Whereas previous researchers have focused on explaining sense of belonging as a major determinant of college student success (e.g., Strayhorn, 2019) or exploring linkages between belonging and key learning outcomes for LGBTQ+ *or* Black student-athletes (e.g., Cooper & Newton, 2021), few studies have focused on examining sense of belonging and campus involvement for student-athletes who are both *Black and LGBTQ+*, hereafter Black LGBTQ+ student-athletes. This is the gap addressed in the present chapter.

Purpose

The purpose of this chapter was to explore the academic and social involvement experiences of Black LGBTQ+ college student-athletes and the role such moments play on their sense of belonging in college. We will use results from a quantitative study to identify promising practices that administrators, faculty, athletic coaches, and others can use to create affirming environments for Black LGBTQ+ student-athletes on- and off-campus. The next section presents a brief summary of the existing literature.

Literature Review

It's estimated that there are over 8,500 sexual minority college student-athletes in the NCAA, according to reports (Coufal, 2018). Quite frankly, the higher education enterprise does not collect or publish national statistics on the number of LGBTQIA2S+ student-athletes of color. This obvious omission must be addressed in future initiatives.

A significant body of research has explored the social experiences of LGBTQ+ college student-athletes' in competitive sports. Previous research reports that some Black LGBTQ+ student-athletes face discrimination, stigma, prejudice, and even forms of violence from college athletic staff, coaches, and teammates (Denison et al., 2021). For instance, during a recent campus visit to a private liberal arts college in Pennsylvania, three Black male football players shared with one of us that they were spit on, pushed, and teased by white coaches, trainers, and players, who may have questioned their spirituality, sexuality, or another private identity. These experiences are highly racialized and often lead to increased feelings of social exclusion and rejection among Black LGBTQ+ student-athletes. Feeling socially isolated, excluded, and rejected by others in team-based spaces where they seek and expect acceptance, camaraderie, and respect may threaten their sense of belonging in college, which is a key determinant of educational success (Strayhorn, 2019).

While prior research is crucial for underscoring the importance of affirming campus spaces for LGBTQ+ student-athletes, there remains a notable gap in understanding the constellation of programs, policies, and *promising practices* that issue a strong sense of belonging for Black LGBTQIA+ college student-athletes. For instance, scholars exploring the social experiences of Black college students tend to emphasize academic- and co-curricular forms of *involvement* such as student government associations, fraternities and sororities (i.e., Black Greek-lettered organizations [BGLOs] in the literature), residence life, and campus gospel choirs, to name a few (Harper & Quaye, 2007; Strayhorn, 2011). LGBTQ scholars, on the other hand, emphasize involvement in queer-identified groups such as student leadership in LGBTQ+ organizations, fraternities/sororities, and service-learning (Rankin et al., 2013), directing much less attention to Black LGBTQ+ college students actively involved in campus-sanctioned sports teams. Even those studying LGBTQ+ student-athletes praise the impact of support groups, anti-bullying initiatives, out/allied staff, and inclusive policies (e.g., codes of conduct) on creating positive, welcoming campus climates for LGBTQ+ college athletes (Rankin & Merson, 2012; Rankin et al., 2013). What's missing are studies that bring these three lines of inquiry together to explore sense of belonging and campus involvement experiences of Black LGBTQ+ student-athletes, with very few exceptions (Ross, 2006).

Lack of attention to this segment of the student population may perpetuate the status quo and limit our evidence-based understanding of the social experiences of such students who represent a largely invisible group, though rising in visibility and voice amid the #BlackLivesMatter and gay rights movements. For instance, recent headlines have called attention to the first openly gay football player at an HBCU, as well as more racially inclusive athletics departments at predominantly white institutions (PWIs). The weight of evidence powerfully suggests a need for more evidence-based practices that hold promise for nurturing a strong sense of belonging in college for Black LGBTQ+ student-athletes. This is the gap addressed by our study that sits at the center of the present chapter.

Our review of the existing literature also turned up a fairly impressive array of doctoral dissertations focusing on various aspects of on- and off-campus experiences for LGBTQ+ college student-athletes of color. For example, Kelley (2019) conducted a phenomenological study of eight LGBQ+ women student-athletes using two semi-structured interviews. She found that some LGBQ+ women student-athletes find it difficult, if not impossible, to separate their gay identity from their athletic identity, especially in light of external factors such as family, society, and media. Other dissertation studies shed light on racial microaggressions (Lee, 2017), activism (Kluch, 2018), and, notably, even staff members' experience with policy application (Hardin, 2021).

We include this summary of dissertation studies for several reasons, one of which is to push back against the conclusion that the existing literature is "remarkably thin" on the experiences of LGBTQ+ college student-athletes of color. To be sure, there's room for much more research on this topic and group. But what does exist is quite new, in keeping with recent calls for more intersectional and critical work—thus, scholars would do well to consider independent research recently published through *ProQuest* and other sources.

With this review in mind, we now present the chapter's guiding, core questions and segue into a fuller discussion of the theoretical framework.

Core Questions

We analyzed survey data to explore two core questions. They include:

1. What are the academic and social involvement experiences of Black LGBTQ+ student-athletes in college?
2. What influence do such campus involvement experiences have on Black LGBTQ+ student-athletes' sense of belonging?

Before describing the study that served as a basis for the recommendations highlighted in this chapter, we provide an overview of our theoretical framework in the next section.

Theoretical Framework | Sense of Belonging

Strayhorn's (2019) sense of belonging model served as the study's theoretical framework. Sense of belonging is defined as "students' perceived social support on campus, a feeling or sensation of connectedness, the experience of mattering or feeling cared about, accepted, respected, valued by, and important to the group or others on campus" (p. 4). Belonging plays an essential role in ensuring safety and security, fostering connections and community, while also engendering student success. Figure 3.1 presents a summary.

Sense of belonging has seven core elements (Strayhorn, 2019). One of them is the basic human need for meaningful connections to specific groups, individuals, or places. Another is the strong desire for interpersonal

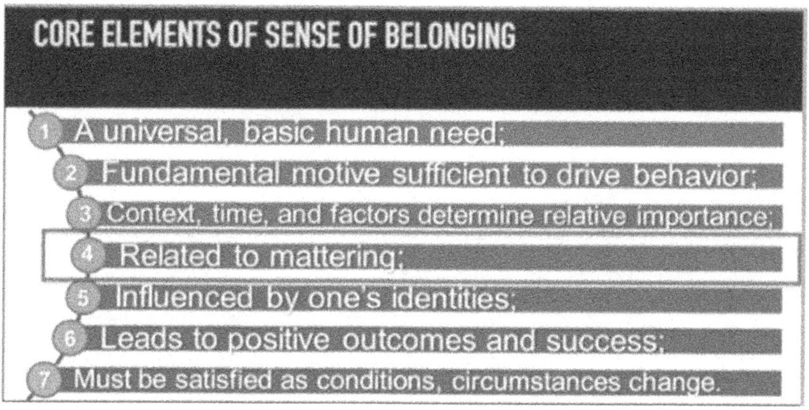

Figure 3.1 Core elements of sense of belonging. Strayhorn, 2019.

relationships, which motivates an individual to do things (i.e., behaviors) that reinforce their connection and integration within the chosen community. Another major element of the model is that belonging is strongly correlated with *mattering*. Mattering is defined as one's experience of feeling valued by others, playing an important role, and adding value to the group (e.g., Schlossberg, 1989). See Figure 3.2 for more.

Prior research on belonging has drawn several conclusions. For example, sense of belonging has been linked to better academic achievement, greater campus engagement, and improved overall well-being (e.g., Rhee, 2008). Moreover, studies have shown that higher levels of perceived belonging correlate with increased self-esteem, greater self-efficacy, and improved academic outcomes, in keeping with Figure 3.1. Belonging scholars emphasize that student success is intricately tied to students' perception of social support from both campus personnel and peers, fostering a stronger connection to the college environment and subsequently increasing college satisfaction (Strayhorn, 2019).

If nothing else, we know from prior research that sense of belonging is a key to educational success for all students, including Black college students (e.g., Strayhorn, 2023), LGBTQ+ students (e.g., Garvey et al., 2019), college-student-athletes (e.g., Gaston Gayles et al., 2018), and herein we explore its importance for Black LGBTQ+ college student-athletes. It's been noted that "involvement in campus sports-related activities [is] positively correlated with sense of belonging in college" (Strayhorn, 2019, p. 147). The next section summarizes the study and presents key findings.

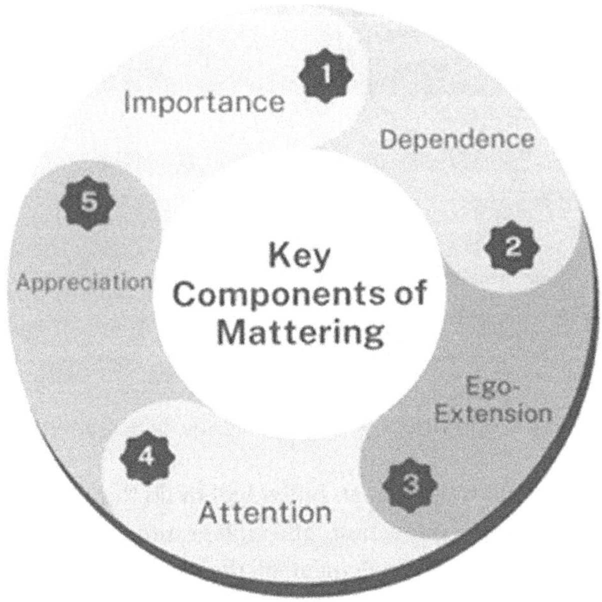

Figure 3.2 Key elements of mattering. Schlossberg, 1989

The Study

To help make sense of the chapter's topic, we used an ex-post facto survey design drawing on information from a large, existing database that's frequently used in college studies, namely the *National Survey of Student Engagement* (NSSE).

Specific criteria were applied to the larger sample to identify eligible participants. We sought respondents who met three criteria: (a) identified as Black, (b) identified as LGBTQ+, *and* (c) reported being a student-athlete. In total, 43 participants met the criteria for the analytic sample. Among Black LGBTQ+ student-athletes in the sample, 79 percent identified as women, 12 percent were members of fraternities/sororities, 2 percent international, and 14 percent self-reported being diagnosed with a disability. The majority (79 percent) lived in an on campus residence hall, while 11 percent lived in an apartment or residence off-campus. In terms of sexual orientation, 1 percent are lesbian, 2 percent are gay, and 5 percent are bisexual, to mention a few.

What We Did | Our Methods

In this exploration of the campus involvement experiences of Black LGBTQ+ student-athletes, we employed a comprehensive approach to our work utilizing NSSE as our primary data source. NSSE is an annual survey administered to first-year and senior students at participating colleges and universities in the United States and Canada. The survey consists of over ninety items designed to assess the extent to which students engage in documented effective educational practices (DEEP) that produce high levels of learning and development. The questionnaire includes a broad range of questions covering various aspects of campus life, such as academic challenges, peer collaborations, faculty interactions, and campus environment perceptions. The survey is distributed to a stratified random sample of students at participating institutions, including historically underrepresented groups such as students of color, student-athletes, veterans, international, and LGBTQ+ students.

For this project, we analyzed data in two stages. First, we prepared data for statistical analysis using a series of (re)coding techniques consistent with the study's conceptual framework, including creating a proxy measure for *sense of belonging* by averaging multiple items on the survey. For instance, one item asked students to rate the nature of their relationships with peers and faculty using a scale, ranging from 1 ("cold, unfriendly, alienation") to 7 ("warm, welcoming, belonging"). Second, we employed descriptive statistics to summarize the sample and Black LGBTQ+ student-athlete's involvement in social experiences on campus. To delve deeper, in keeping with Chayla's story that opened the chapter, we used multivariate statistics, namely regression analysis, to quantify the relationship between specific campus involvement experiences (e.g., service-learning, clubs) and sense of belonging to develop a more nuanced portrait of this largely unseen student population.

What We Found | Our Results

We used seventeen survey items organized into three major categories to explore Black LGBTQ+ student-athletes' campus involvement. Five items focused on the frequency of students' discussions and interactions with others on campus. Results were quite revealing, showing that Black LGBTQ+ student-athletes rarely, if ever, talk with faculty about their career plans but spend much more time having discussions with people of other races. Table 3.1 presents a summary.

We used seven other items to measure Black LGBTQ+ student-athletes' engagement in high-impact practices (HIPs). For instance, items measured whether they had completed (or were completing) an internship, study abroad, learning community, and service learning, to name a few. Results were telling—72 percent of Black LGBTQ+ student-athletes reported involvement in *service learning* and 17 percent in *campus leadership*, but just 8 percent in study abroad. Table 3.2 presents a full summary.

A final set of items tracked how much time Black LGBTQ+ student-athletes spend weekly on social activities. For instance, results show that our participants devoted considerably more time to co-curricular activities and hanging out with friends than working on- or off-campus for pay. Table 3.3 presents a summary.

We regressed the seventeen survey items on sense of belonging to study the influence of campus involvement on this outcome for Black LGBTQ+ student-athletes. In short, the regression was significant, $F\ (17,37) = 2.04$, $p < 0.10$. Three variables met our threshold for statistical significance ($p < 0.10$), and three other variables *approached* statistical significance. Five

Table 3.1 *Descriptive Results for Black LGBTQ+ Student-athletes' Campus Involvement with Others*

Survey Item	*M*	SD
Talked about career plans with a faculty member	2.37	1.09
Had discussions with people of a race or ethnicity other than you own	3.24	0.88
Had discussions with people from an economic background other than your own	3.21	0.87
Had discussions with people with religious beliefs other than your own	3.05	0.88
Had discussions with people with political views other than your own	2.81	0.86

Note. Survey items measure the frequency of respondents' involvement in campus experiences (e.g., discussions) with others, using a range of 1 (never) to 4 (very often). *M* = mean. *SD* = standard deviation.

Table 3.2 *Descriptive Results for Black LGBTQ+ Student-athlete's Campus Involvement*

Survey Item	*M*	*SD*
Internship	0.19	0.39
Leadership	0.17	0.38
Learning community	0.24	0.43
Study abroad	0.08	0.27
Faculty research	0.12	0.33
Capstone	0.23	0.43
Service learning	0.72	0.45

Note. Survey item measures the proportion of respondents who indicated "done/complete" or "in progress." *M* = mean. *SD* = standard deviation.

Table 3.3 *Descriptive Results for Black LGBTQ+ Student-athlete's Campus Involvement*

Survey Item	M	SD
Co-curricular activities	12.90	8.46
Working on campus	4.70	6.76
Working off-campus	4.19	8.13
Community service	4.33	7.01
Relaxing with friends	11.78	10.24

Note. Survey item estimates hours per week that respondents devote to a range of college activities. *M* = mean. *SD* = standard deviation.

will guide our discussion and recommendations in the sections that follow. These five include time spent (1) relaxing with friends, (2) doing co-curricular activities, (3) volunteering through community service, (4) interacting with people holding different political views, and (5) working on campus.

Discussion | Our Points

If our count is correct, we're over 4,000 words into this book chapter and just a few short sections away from its end. So, what's the main point? We've got several that relate to the overall aims of this book. First, contrary to popular belief, not all Black students are the same, in keeping with

Harper's (2008) published observation about Black men in college. But, guess what? Neither are all LGBTQ+ students or all student-athletes! Facts. We must stop forcing students into tight, restrictive boxes that reduce the beauty of their complex humanity into single categories or labels. Our study sheds light on a largely invisible and wholly under investigated student population—those who are at all times *Black and LGBTQ+ and student-athletes and* so much more than we can ever imagine. Consider our sample of Black LGBTQ+ student-athletes. They're men and women, US-born and international students, living on- and off-campus, and over 14 percent self-reported living with a disability. Friends, they are as diverse as the institutions they attend. There's no question that this chapter fills a noticeable gap in the literature with so few published studies on Black LGBTQ+ college student-athletes. Much more research is warranted in the future. We highly encourage *any* graduate students reading this chapter to make this topic the focus of your thesis, dissertation, or summer research project immediately . . . please and thank you.

Our findings are not entirely unique. Like Rankin and her colleagues (e.g., Rankin & Merson, 2012; Rankin et al., 2013), we found evidence supporting the fact that LGBTQ+ students of color do engage with faculty, staff, and peers whose backgrounds differ from their own, and the same holds true for Black LGBTQ+ student-athletes. However, they don't interact with everyone the same, in terms of the frequency and nature of such interactions (e.g., academic vs. social). Our analysis shows that time devoted to high-impact practices can make or break Black LGBTQ+ student-athletes' sense of belonging on campus. While study abroad and capstone projects exert little influence on the extent to which they feel like they matter and belong in college, campus involvement experiences seem to "punch above their weight," especially time spent weekly in co-curricular activities, hanging out with friends, and working on campus for pay. The latter two actually have an inverse relationship with Black LGBTQ+ student-athletes' sense of belonging, perhaps reflecting the negative impact of having to hide or conceal one's sexuality. Indeed, some forms of campus involvement inhibit students' sense of belonging. This can happen when hanging out with unaccepting peers and working in unsupportive environments, especially for student-athletes, LGBTQ+ folx, and Black LGBTQ+ student-athletes who are "both at all times," quoting Chayla's words.

But our study's not a repeat of the past—we offer some fresh perspectives and new takes on old issues. For instance, Black LGBTQ+ student-athletes in our study had limited discussions with others who hold different political views and religious beliefs. Intuitively, this makes sense, right?! This may be due to their multiple dimensions of identity and strong polarizing perspectives on sensitive issues such as race (especially anti-Blackness), sexuality, and even more recently the hotly contested "Pay for Play" debate. Most of us are motivated—even raised—to avoid contentious, divisive, and difficult conversations "at the dinner table," so to speak. That same wisdom may hold true here, acting as a barrier between Black LGBTQ+ student-athletes and their campus peers. Let's be honest though—some students avoid such conversations as a way of intentionally protecting themselves from the harm of racist, sexist, or homophobic opinions that threaten their safety and security. Still, a long line of research clearly suggests that well-structured, difficult conversations can produce significant growth and development (Gayle et al., 2013; Koopman & Seliga, 2021), even among student-athletes (Fraley et al., 2020). As educators, we must find ways to help support all students safely and courageously through these catalyzing moments both inside and outside the classroom.

In addition, findings reveal low participation rates among Black LGBTQ+ student-athletes in key co-curricular opportunities such as internships, leadership roles, study-abroad programs, and faculty-guided research. Of course, we recognize these students lead incredibly demanding lives between their academics and sports. However, facilitating stronger engagement with these high-impact activities could greatly enrich Black LGBTQ+ athletes' persistence and overall student experience. More needs to be done to provide targeted support in helping interested athletes take advantage of such experiences, in light of their time constraints. Study-abroad partnerships might be established between professional sports associations, the NCAA, PRIDE groups, and community organizations that may speak to the unique interests of some Black LGBTQ+ student-athletes. For example, an institution might work with global agencies to bring intramural sports to LGBTQ+ youth in underdeveloped and developing countries. With attentiveness to Black LGBTQ+ student-athletes' unique circumstances, institutions can open more doors for them to reap the substantial benefits of engaging deeply both inside and outside the classroom. We will comment on this more in the recommendations section.

A final point deserves mention before pivoting to the last and final part of this chapter. In our study, we explore the multifaceted lives of Black LGBTQ+ student-athletes in ways that embrace (not deny) their complex, intersectional identities and the myriad roles and responsibilities they hold far beyond the sports arena. One thing's clear and that is these students do not live their lives within the confines of their athletic identity only. Rather, they embody a diverse array of roles that contribute significantly to their personal development and sense of belonging. We, as educators, can harness the transformative power of these experiences, *if and only if* we take time to truly see them *as they are.*

Our findings underscore what so many have said to us in interviews and focus groups—that Black LGBTQ+ student-athletes are indeed "more than just athletes." Look back at our results and tables. Many are roommates, sharing living quarters on- and off-campus where they can build lasting friendships, master conflict resolution, and, yes, even engage people whose backgrounds and opinions are different. Beyond living spaces, Black LGBTQ+ student-athletes engage in academic collaborations that further their intellectual pursuits. They work with faculty members on research projects, volunteer through community service, log clinical hours, hold internships, and a select few study abroad or engage in short-term study away.

Leadership is another domain where Black LGBTQ+ student-athletes shine, according to our study. Many take on pivotal roles in campus clubs and organizations, steering efforts to improve campus climate, address community concerns, and help live out the institution's mission. Their leadership seems to extend to organizing events, leading discussions, and advocating for causes that likely resonate with aspects of their identities and core values. Think back to Chayla's story and the transformative role that involvement in *Shades* and *M2M* played for her.

Our study affirms what we've known for some time—campus involvement matters and makes a difference in terms of college students' learning and development (Astin, 1999). Like early theorists and writers since, we found support for perspectives that posit involvement as having both quantitative and qualitative features to it *and* that the amount of students' learning and development associated with a specific campus program or practice is directly proportional to the degree and nature of their involvement. Involvement in campus clubs, organizations, service-learning initiatives, and fraternities/sororities is important for Black LGBTQ+ student-athletes. The time and type of involvement significantly shapes their perceptions of mattering and membership. Another important ingredient of Astin's involvement theory is the idea that time or energy invested in *one activity* represents a reduction in the time and energy available for other activities. For instance, it may be the case that sports training, competing, practicing, studying, and on campus work leave little to no time for Black LGBTQ+ student-athletes to engage in study abroad, faculty-led research, campus leadership, or out-of-class political conversations. Faculty advisors, coaches, and trainers should consider these results when working with such students. Find ways to encourage a healthy dose of "sports-life balance," marked by time in the gym, on the field, but also in the lab, with friends, and abroad.

Perhaps the most important thing we can do with all that we've written in this piece so far is draw upon our findings to make strong recommendations for future research, policy, and practice. We turn our attention to these goals in the next section.

Recommendations

Building upon the key findings from our comprehensive analysis of Black LGBTQ+ student-athletes, we offer a series of major recommendations designed to leverage these insights for future research/theory, policy, and practice. These recommendations aim to address some of the challenges and opportunities identified earlier, setting a path forward for meaningful change and campus improvements.

Research/Theory

- Future researchers should explore the issue of Black LGBTQ+ student-athletes' campus involvement and sense of belonging using diverse methods such as longitudinal designs, qualitative approaches (e.g., interviews, document analysis), or innovative tools like portraiture.

Figure 3.3 Belonging visual analysis. Strayhorn, 2024.

- Like so many others, we provide support herein that affirms sense of belonging theory (Strayhorn, 2019), even for Black LGBTQ+ student-athletes. Scholars might work to develop interdisciplinary, intersectional frames that integrate insights from psychology, sociology, education, LGBT studies, and other relevant fields to further explore this topic. Below we illustrate the possibility of this point by mapping a few of Chayla's comments on an integrated model of mattering and belonging (Figure 3.3).

Policy

- Ensure that athletic departments have inclusive policies and nondiscrimination statements that explicitly address race, sexual orientation, and gender identity.
- Establish partnerships with LGBTQ+ organizations or advocacy groups to inform and enhance the development of equitable policies that specifically address the needs of LGBTQ+ student-athletes of color.
- Revise existing or formulate new policies that govern study-abroad experiences including how long students visit abroad, the types of

experiences, and even funding mechanisms that help defray the expensive costs for college students.

Practices and Programs

- Establish mentoring programs that connect Black LGBTQ+ student-athletes with mentors who appreciate, honor, and understand their unique lived experiences, including, for instance, faculty, work supervisors, coaches, and on campus peers. Given the importance of representation *in* belonging, it may be helpful to actively recruit diverse mentors who share students' core identities in common.
- Implement visibility campaigns that celebrate and highlight the achievements and contributions of Black LGBTQ+ student-athletes.
- Create educational initiatives that raise awareness about the experiences of Black LGBTQ+ individuals, including student-athletes, such as book clubs focused on volumes authored by members of the community, film series, and anti-bullying programs (Rankin et al., 2013).
- More visible and vocal pro-LGBTQ+ stances from those in leadership positions, especially coaches, athletic directors, and trainers.

Conclusion | Our Sound Off

It is our collective hope that this chapter will find its way into the hands of many who want to learn more about the lived experiences of Black LGBTQ+ student-athletes, including but not limited to campus presidents, vice presidents, athletic directors, faculty, student affairs staff, and trustees, to name a few. But we also hope that this work circles back to affirm, uplift, and inspire those who sit at the center of this matter—Black LGBTQ+ student-athletes themselves. Folx, like Chayla, whose story inspired the opening segment of this chapter. Sis, we heard you, loud and clear. You *are* "more than an athlete!" So to anyone who needs to hear it, say this: *I matter. I am enough. I belong here, just as I am.* Now, rinse and repeat until you believe it as much as we do.

References

Anderson, A. R., Stokowski, S., Smith, C. M., & Turk, M. R. (2023). "You have to validate it": Experiences of female sexual minority student-athletes. *Journal of Homosexuality, 70*(3), 497–518.

Astin, A. W. (1999). Student involvement: A developmental theory for higher education. *Journal of College Student Development, 40*(5), 518–529. file:///E:/My%20Documents/My%20Research/Involvement/AstinInvolvement.pdf

Brody, E., Scott, D. T., & Pariera, K. L. (2022). LGBTQ+ collegiate athletes and the double bind: insights from the experiences of out varsity athletes. *International Journal of Communication, 16*, 21.

Carter-Francique, A. R. (2018). Is excellence inclusive? The benefits of fostering Black female college athlete's sense of belonging. *Journal of Higher Education Athletics & Innovation, 1*(3), 48.

Cooper, J. N., & Newton, A. (2021). Black female college athletes' sense of belonging at a Historically Black College and University (HBCU). *Journal of Negro Education, 90*(1), 71–83.

Coufal, T. (2018). *Inclusion of LGBTQ student-athletes on NCAA sport teams: Perspectives from student-athletes* (Doctoral dissertation), The University of the Rockies.

Cunningham, G. B. (2015). Creating and sustaining workplace cultures supportive of LGBT employees in college athletics. *Journal of Sport Management, 29*(4), 426–442.

Denison, E., Bevan, N., & Jeanes, R. (2021). Reviewing evidence of LGBTQ+ discrimination and exclusion in sport. *Sport Management Review, 24*(3), 389–409.

Fraley, T., Warner, S., Wilson, C., Catalano, M., & Jones, G. (2020). Tackling difficult conversations: Student-athletes, mental health, and emerging technology. *Journal of Athlete Development and Exercise, 2*(2), 103–116. https://doi.org/10.25035/jade.02.02.03

Garvey, J. C., Mobley Jr, S. D., Summerville, K. S., & Moore, G. T. (2019). Queer and trans* students of color: Navigating identity disclosure and college contexts. *The Journal of Higher Education, 90*(1), 150–178.

Gayle, B. M, Cortez, D., & Preiss, R. W. (2013). Safe spaces, difficult dialogues, and critical thinking. *International Journal of the Scholarship of Teaching & Learning, 7*(2), Article 5. https://doi.org/10.20429/ijsotl.2013.070205

Gayles, J. G., Crandall, R., & Morin, S. (2018). Student-athletes' sense of belonging: Background characteristics, student involvement, and campus climate. *The International Journal of Sport and Society*, *9*(1), 23.

Hardin, B. M. (2021). Intercollegiate Athletic Department Staff Members' Lived Experiences with Policy Implementation for Trans Student Athletes (Doctoral dissertation, Mercer University).

Harper, S. R., & Nichols, A. H. (2008). Are they not all the same? Racial heterogeneity among Black male undergraduates. *Journal of College Student Development, 49*(3), 199–214.

Harper, S. R., & Quaye, S. J. (2007). Student organizations as venues for black identity expression and development among african American male student leaders. *Journal of College Student Development*, *48*, 127–144.

Havey, N. (2021). Untapped potential: Understanding how LGBQ students use dating applications to explore, develop, and learn about their sexual identities. *Journal of Women and Gender in Higher Education*, *14*(3), 324–341.

Kelley, E. A. (2019). *"I can't separate me being gay and me being athlete": A phenomenological study of LGBQ+ women student-athletes* (Publication No. 27664709) [Doctoral dissertation, University of Massachusetts, Boston]. ProQuest Dissertations & Theses Global.

King, K. R. (2017). Three waves of gay male athlete coming out narratives. *Quarterly Journal of Speech*, *103*(4), 372–394.

Kluch, Y. (2018). More Than an Athlete: A Qualitative Examination of Activist Identities Among NCAA Division I Student-Athletes (Doctoral dissertation, Bowling Green State University).

Koopman, S., & Seliga, L. (2021). Teaching peace by using nonviolent communication for difficult conversations in the college classroom. *Peace & Conflict Studies*, *27*(3), Article 2. https://doi.org/10.46743/1082-7307/2021.1692

Lee, S. M. (2017). Student-athletes' experiences with racial microaggressions in sport: A Foucauldian discourse analysis. West Virginia University.

Newhall, K. E., & Buzuvis, E. E. (2008). (e) Racing Jennifer Harris: Sexuality and race, law and discourse in Harris v. Portland. *Journal of Sport and Social Issues*, *32*, 345–368.

Ottenritter, N. (2012). Crafting a caring and inclusive environment for LGBTQ community college students, faculty, and staff. *Community College Journal of Research and Practice*, *36*(7), 531–538.

Rankin, S., & Merson, D. (2012). *Campus Pride 2012 LGBTQ national college athlete report*. Campus Pride.

Rankin, S. R., Hesp, G. A., & Weber, G. N. (2013). Experiences and perceptions of gay and bisexual fraternity members from 1960 to 2007: A cohort analysis. *Journal of College Student Development, 54*(6), 570–590.

Rhee, B. (2008). Institutional climate and student departure: A multinomial multilevel modeling approach. *The Review of Higher Education, 31*(2), 161–183.

Ross, J., R. (2006). *Triple threat: My journey as a Black Lesbian Athlete in seatch of additional black lesbian student-athletes* (Unpublished master's thesis). University of Tennessee, Knoxville

Schlossberg, N. K. (1989). Marginality and mattering: Key issues in building community. *New Directions for Student Services, 48*(1), 5–15.

Stokowski, S., & O'Donnell, S. (2022). Rethinking disability inclusion in intercollegiate athletics: Examining the NCAA's mission and priorities. *Sports Innovation Journal, SI*, 41–54. https://doi.org/10.18060/26004

Strayhorn, T., L. (2011). Singing in a foreign land: An exploratory study of gospel choir participation among African American undergraduates at a predominantly white institution. *Journal of College Student Development, 52*(2), 137–153.

Strayhorn, T. L. (2019). *College students' sense of belonging: A key to educational success for all students*. Routledge.

Strayhorn, T. L. (2023). Estimating differences in the effects of living-learning community participation on Black students' sense of belonging at predominantly White and historically Black colleges and universities. *Journal of College Student Development, 64*(2), 225–230.

Turk, M. R., Stokowski, S. E., & Dittmore, S. W. (2019). "Don't be open or tell anyone": Inclusion of sexual minority college athletes. *Journal of Issues in Intercollegiate Athletics, 12*(1), 564–589.

Wolf-Wendel, L., Bajaj, A., & Spriggs, T. (2008). Responding to the needs of lesbian, gay, and bisexual student-athletes and their team members. *NACADA Monograph Series, 18*, 31–36.

4

"They Just So Happen to Be Born in the Right Family"

A Story of Elitism on an HBCU

Jorge Burmicky and Kathleen Rzucidlo

Chapter Outline

Historically Black Colleges and Universities (HBCUs) are known for providing racially and culturally affirming postsecondary spaces to Black students across the country (Palmer & Williams, 2021; Williams et al., 2019). Despite many institutions reporting enrollment declines since the onset of the Covid-19 pandemic, HBCUs have found themselves in what educational leaders and policy advocates have framed as an "enrollment renaissance" (Green, 2022, para 6), with record-levels of Black Americans choosing HBCUs. Furthermore, prominent HBCUs are attracting top-tier Black high school graduates at unparalleled rates (Green, 2022; K. L. Williams et al., 2021). As highlighted in Burmicky et al. Burmicky et al. (2022), Black students are seeking HBCUs because most predominantly white institutions (PWIs) are not able to provide the much-needed culturally and racially affirming educational spaces they deserve.

Scholars have studied campus involvement and student experiences at HBCUs through a myriad of approaches (Miller et al., 2021; Palmer & Maramba, 2015; Strayhorn & Terrell, 2010). Studies such as Williams and colleagues (2019) challenged deficit notions about HBCUs by providing assets-based counternarratives from presidents at these institutions. Their study underlined the ways in which HBCUs have been able to tap the potential of Black students despite having very limited financial resources. Williams and colleagues (2021) shed light on why Black students are choosing HBCUs at higher rates than ever before. By bringing attention to the racial climate of the United States after the election of a president that publicly embraced racism, white supremacy, and populism for political gain (see Charlottesville aftermath in Howard-Woods et al., 2019), Williams and colleagues provided tangible examples of why Black students do not always feel safe leaving home for college because "of their identity and skin color" (p. 807) , and unpacked why HBCUs are perceived as safer and more supportive than PWIs.

Prior research covers other points. For example, Winkle-Wagner and McCoy (2018) examined the experiences of STEM students of color and faculty at a PWI and an HBCU. They concluded that students of color at HBCUs felt more supported than their peers at PWIs, and perceived STEM disciplines at HBCUs to be more diverse and inclusive as a result of their interactions with faculty. Overall, an underlying theme across these studies is that HBCUs provide a familial approach to the intellectual, emotional, and social well-being of Black students. Moreover, many of these studies stressed the important role that HBCU faculty and staff play in making students feel safe and accepted on campus. Namely, as Strayhorn (2019) emphasized, race matters when it comes to cultivating sense of belonging, and for too long mainstream media has chosen not to report on how HBCUs have excelled at educating communities that have been neglected for centuries by American society and PWIs at large.

Because the Covid-19 pandemic disrupted so much of everyday life, it is critical to understand the student experiences of HBCUs, especially at a time when racial tensions in the United States are high (Williams et al., 2021). The inexcusable killings of George Floyd, Breonna Taylor, Ahmaud Arbery, and countless others have left many in our nation wondering why we continue to allow police brutality against Black Americans at such alarming rates. As documented by Green (2022), incoming college students are not willing to accept this, and they have turned to HBCUs as nurturing spaces where they can thrive intellectually while not having to worry about their safety.

Given this imperative and rising popularity of HBCUs, it is critical to add scholarly depth to how students find sense of belonging and involvement on these campuses. We define sense of belonging as a basic human need that, within the context of colleges and universities, is often linked to being a valued member of the campus community as a result of social, emotional, physical, and intellectual togetherness (Strayhorn, 2023). No campus is perfect, and HBCUs face different challenges than their PWI peers. For example, HBCUs have been disproportionately impacted by chronic disinvestment and long-standing structural inequities compared to their PWI peers (Harris, 2021; Strayhorn, 2022). Though many prominent HBCUs have benefited from enrollment spikes in recent years, not all HBCUs have. Furthermore, although HBCUs enroll high percentages of first-generation, working-class, and Pell-recipient Black students (Strayhorn, 2021), some also enroll highly affluent legacy students, often leading to complex social dynamics fueled by elitism and social hierarchies on campuses that were intended to serve already marginalized students (Taylor, 2008). Thus, it seems reasonable to expect a spectrum of mattering and sense of belonging experiences across students attending HBCUs.

Drawing from our ongoing research on HBCU mattering and belonging (see Burmicky et al., 2022), the purpose of this chapter is to elaborate on the role that elitism plays in the campus involvement and sense of belonging experiences of undergraduate students at an HBCU. Using interview and focus group data, we apply a composite narrative approach to depict the story of an undergraduate student at a private, selective

HBCU. Through storytelling, we call attention to this student's quest to belong while navigating elitism on campus.

Background of This Chapter

In fall 2021, we wrote a grant proposal to explore how undergraduate students at our campus found meaningful opportunities for campus involvement. At that time, the Covid-19 pandemic permeated every aspect of life, with thousands of daily deaths reported worldwide. We were interested in understanding how students connected with their campus community amid a global health crisis. Most of us were wrestling with feelings of isolation while assessing our levels of risk for exposure to the deadly virus. Face coverings and proof of vaccination were required for everyone on campus.

As former student affairs professionals, we were drawn to understanding how students connected with their campus in such a tumultuous time. Jorge was a new tenure-track faculty member in higher education, and Kathleen—or "K" for short—was a new graduate student in higher education. Being new to campus brought a sense of excitement and curiosity to studying the experiences of undergraduate students in our new academic home. We also wanted to explore the types of campus involvement opportunities that were afforded to students, especially since many campuses had pivoted to offering almost all student support services remotely to mitigate risk of Covid-19 exposure.

In spring 2022, we were awarded a grant by the NACA Foundation[1] to begin our study. Like most studies, our research questions evolved as we began to engage with the study and its participants. For example, while doing data collection, students—just like us—were still making sense of the impact of the latest Covid-19 subvariant, Omicron. By talking to participants, we learned that students navigated their pandemic circumstances very differently. Some were eager to resume activities in person, while others were more hesitant and had already adjusted their

---

[1]For more information about the NACA Foundation, see here: https://www.naca.org/Foundation/Pages/default.aspx. The name of the funded study is "A Snapshot of Campus Involvement in the COVID-19 Pandemic: An HBCU-based Case Study."

college plans to stay remote long-term. Some of these themes were highlighted in Burmicky et al. (2022), which focused on HBCU undergraduate student barriers and challenges for getting involved on campus. As we learned more about students' sense of belonging, a strong sub-theme emerged across the data: elitism. Students described elitism as a type of social hierarchy defined by social economic status, family name, and their social network (Burmicky et al., 2022). We were pulled into this finding as we were aware that scholarship on elitism and HBCU campuses is limited (Taylor, 2008).

We have had the opportunity to present our findings at the Association for the Study of Higher Education (ASHE) annual conference, professional development workshops, and to senior leadership on campus, including our vice president for student affairs. Given the high interest we have received about the topic of elitism on campus, we decided to use this book chapter as the ideal platform to further unpack this finding. It is important to note that although elitism is the main topic of discussion in this chapter, we used this opportunity to narrate Jessie's journey to college, our composite narrative character. Before discussing elitism, we recognize the need to explain her overall collegiate experiences that offer insights to elitism at her campus.

Methodology

This study employed a qualitative single case study design to explore the experiences of undergraduate students at one campus (Yin, 2009). This led us to bound our study by physical location and type of student (Stake, 2008). By virtue of having access to participants, we chose a private research HBCU. Being focused on one HBCU allowed us to fully immerse ourselves in the campus culture, as well as to have access to a diverse group of participants.

This study gathered data from seventeen individual interviews and one focus group with three students, totaling twenty participants. Our interview and focus group protocols were focused on getting a firm grip on how students got involved on campus while negotiating the struggles that came with going to college during a global pandemic. Interview data collection took place via Zoom, and each interview lasted approximately thirty to sixty minutes. The focus group took place in person and lasted approximately sixty minutes. All data were transcribed by an external transcription service verbatim for data analysis purposes (Saldaña, 2011).

For data analysis, we read transcripts line-by-line to facilitate open coding. We used a data analysis software (Dedoose) to help us manage large amounts of data and access coding tools. Our open coding process involved developing a codebook with words and phrases rooted in our line-by-line transcript reading. We then moved to axial coding (Saldaña, 2011). Axial coding involved meeting regularly during the data analysis stages to group our codes into categories (Miles et al., 2014). After categorizing, we used the 3D word cloud feature of Dedoose to help us identify patterns within these categories. We used emerging patterns to draft our findings by discussing them as a group to ensure intercoder reliability (Miles et al., 2014). It is important to note that our research team is composed of five members, although only two authors wrote this chapter. All members of the research team participated in data collection and analysis, but not all chose to write for this piece due to time constraints and professional commitments.

After identifying the findings, we met to discuss how we wanted to further explore elitism in this book chapter. Because we wanted to effectively communicate the texture of this campus within the context of elitism, we turned to composite narrative methodology. Composite narrative was a compelling way to communicate our research because it allows for the use of interview and focus group data to tell a single story (Cook, 2013; Willis, 2019).

To build our composite, we exported all excerpts that discussed elitism. The quotes that we used for our composite came directly from these excerpts, which we highlighted in bold. All details, including how circumstances evolved and any paraphrasing of discussions were taken directly from our data (Willis, 2019). To add texture and context to our composite, we relied on our own experiences as bone fide members of this campus. In addition, we leveraged our own exposure to informal interactions with undergraduate students, social media forums related to this campus, campus events, and our own lived experiences as a professor and graduate student at this campus (Cook, 2013). This process led us to developing Jessica "Jessie" Jones, our composite character whose story is narrated using everyday, accessible student language. We summarized our methodology process in.

The Story of Jessica "Jessie" Jones

August 22, 2022

Dear Diary,
Today's the day!! It's finally move-in day after a year of online school. I packed up the car with mom and dad to drive up to campus on Thursday, we drove up from Atlanta all day Friday and I am just so excited to come back to campus.

Jessie Jones was admitted to Mid-Atlantic University (MAU), a private HBCU in the Mid-Atlantic region in the fall of 2019. It was her senior year of high school which would end up being interrupted by the COVID-19 pandemic. MAU was her top choice and being the first in her family to be admitted and attend college was a big deal. Though her parents did not attend college, they were adamant about her attending an HBCU. Coming from Atlanta, she knew all about Spelman, Morehouse, Morris Brown and Clark Atlanta University, and it was a no-brainer to attend an HBCU. Jessie's decision to move far away for college was unusual; most of her friends chose colleges nearby. However, they all had their first year together at home as instruction was moved remotely. Jessie's first year of college took place from her bedroom, living room, coffee shop and anywhere her phone took her as she tuned in via Zoom.

Jessie's mom turns around in the passenger seat as they pull onto campus to say, "I can't believe I'm *really* moving my baby into college!" It didn't feel as real when she was simply enrolled in college, but still living at home and in Atlanta. Now it's real.

September 3, 2022

Dear Diary,
I just love this campus! **When you walk outside to just see yourself in all these people, it is just amazing. I feel like I should be here . . . more than my other friends describe at their other schools. They sort of feel uncomfortable, from my interpretation of what they're saying. I'm so glad I chose an HBCU.** My roommate Michele, "Meech" for short, is really dope, she's from Brooklyn. But we haven't met too many other people outside of our group from orientation. I am really looking forward to meeting more people. Stay tuned Diary!

"Wait? You're where? Where is that? Raise your hand up!" Jessie says while on the phone as she walks toward the library to find the organization fair while looking for her roommate in a crowd. From a distance you can hear Meech shout, "Jessie!! I see you!" As they walk toward each other, a group of students build around individuals wearing pink and green, red and white, blue and gold separating the roommates while showing them what just a few of the organizations at MAU are about. Jessie is captivated by the vision of these young women in their pearls, strolling[2] and enjoying every moment with their sorority sisters. She has to know more. After the strolling ends, the roommates link arms and walk around the terrace looking at all of the campus organizations available to them.

A few weeks later, Jessie, Meech and their neighbor Ayo, an international student from Nigeria, walk into Jessie and Meech's dorm room. Jessie lets out a deep sigh and throws herself on her bed, "how is it that there is so much going on around campus *supposedly*, according to Instagram, but I feel like I never hear about anything?" Jessie sighs and takes her gaze away from her phone and looks across her dorm room to Meech who responds, **"I feel like I probably get, I don't know, 100 to 200 emails every single day. I don't look at half of them, some of them are useful because a lot of them are from *Handshake*,[3] but for the most part it's just additional stuff. It gets overwhelming for me honestly**. Even when I go it feels like everyone already has their people and I stand out like a store thumb." Ayo adds, **"It's hard enough trying to make new friends and network, but I sometimes still feel like I'm in a completely new and different environment as an international student . . .** and it's already October, homecoming is around the corner, and we don't even know what's going on with that."

Jessie pops up from her bed, "Y'all, that's going to be our time! We have to make sure to go to as much stuff as we can. Get really cute outfits and be in the mix. We CANNOT miss our first HBCU homecoming." Ayo rolls her eyes, "With what money, Jessie? Everyone here walks around with

---

[2]Strolling can be defined as a synchronized dance typically performed in a line where members of the same organization following a designated leader through the space, can also be referred to as party walking (or hopping in the case of members of Omega Psi Phi Fraternity) (Smith, 2015).

[3]**Handshake is an application used by college campuses to connect students to career opportunities. For more information, see** https://joinhandshake.com/. **This is not an endorsement of this application.**

their Telfar bags, Yeezy slides and all these other Black designers, I can't keep up with the everyday fashion show. It's starting to feel very expensive just walking to class." Meech adds in, "maybe we can go thrifting and be cute, vintage HBCU girlies." The mood in the room shifts from feeling discouraged to beginning to get a little excited with homecoming around the corner.

> October 23, 2022
>
> Dear Diary,
> I can't even make this up. Me, Meech and Ayo have been saving up for homecoming. We woke up so early to try to get tickets for the fashion show and step show and they were sold out before we even got to the window! Meech even skipped her 9:00 am class! I'm so upset, **there's a limited amount of tickets and it's really first come first serve. I mean, it's not their fault that they have a limited amount of space. Everybody can't go, I guess.** It just sucks. This wasn't how I saw homecoming week going. Sometimes I feel like this isn't how I saw college going either.

It's November, but oddly warm outside, while we briefly ignore climate change, a warm day at Mid-Atlantic is the perfect excuse to come outside and sit on the yard. The yard on a nice day instantly becomes a fashion show, social, mixer, people-watching cluster of Black excellence. "It's almost like a day party right outside of the fine arts building, hurry up!" Jessie hangs up the phone and waits for Meech and Ayo to make their way to the steps. Not long after the other girls joined their friend, the yard attracted large crowds. Everyone was there. The girls all look around when Meech says," I wonder what it feels like . . . " Jessie turns her head from people watching, "what what feels like?" Meech continues, "I don't know, to just go here and just, know everything. Like her over there" she points over toward the other side of the yard to a girl walking through campus and waving or saying hi to what seems like everyone, "her mom and dad both pledged and met here in the 90's and most of her siblings and cousins went here too . . . she makes it look so easy."

> November 1, 2022
>
> Dear Diary,
> Legacies, we all know it's important to leave a legacy behind in life, but imagine being the kid that gets to benefit immediately from their parent's legacy. There's this girl, she's in my Econ 101 class. Her life just looks perfect

> on social media and real life. We saw her on the yard today, her hair perfect in long knotless braids, flawless makeup . . . or skin, it's probably just her skin, ugh, the mini Telfar bag, Essentials sweatsuit and mini Ugg boots. Her parents went here in the 90s- her mom was Miss Mid Atlantic, and her dad was captain of the basketball team. It's the perfect college love story we all hope for. She's involved in student government, step master for her residence hall's step team and is probably going to rush her mom's sorority too, of course she'll get picked. Do legacies ever not get picked? **I feel like there's lots of undertones of elitism on this campus. I used to hear people talking about it before I got here, and I didn't understand, but now it's like oh, this is what you guys were talking about.**

"My JJ!" A high pitched voice shrieks from the other side of the parking lot, Jessie's mom is sprinting the short distance toward her baby girl enthusiastically saying, "these last weeks have felt like years, how is my college girl?" Jessie responds, trying to just get in the car as fast as possible, "I'm good mom! How are you?" Jessie's mom looks at her daughter slightly befuddled, "Just good? You don't want to show me around campus or introduce me to all of your new college friends? Not even lunch?" "Mom, I just . . . can we just leave?" Jessie thought to herself, what new college friends? **It's so overwhelming to get involved. I feel like a lot of things here are gate kept and that makes it hard for people to meet other people.** Her mom looks at her shocked, where was her social butterfly of a daughter she dropped off just a few weeks ago? Jessie continues, ". . . some days it feels like I should have just stayed on Zoom. I just need a break, we can go to lunch, but can we go somewhere a bit further away from campus?" Jessie's mom nods, and they hit the highway while a very quiet Jessie rides along looking out the window until they finally pick a restaurant outside of the city.

"Baby, tell me more about what you're feeling?" Jessie lets out a deep sigh as she stares into her diner coffee cup, "I don't know mom, I just thought college would be different. **Being an [MAU] student off campus, it means so much like, 'Oh my gosh, you go to [MAU]??' On campus, it's more so, you go to [MAU], so do I. What else? What are you a part of? What have I seen you in? I know your name. Who do I know it through? You know them? You know everybody? The networking aspect is very important, and it can be a little cliquey** and I'm not doing too good at it." **People are obsessed with the idea of selectivity and a perfect example is organizations where they're testing you and drilling**

you to get into an organization that is about fostering a safe space for students, and stuff like that, it's really backwards to me, and I see that type of mentality in a lot of unnecessary spaces. It's just very elitist and I feel like I should just go somewhere else."

Jessie's mom hugs her coffee cup just a little tighter with her hands before she puts it down and extends her hand across the dinner tabletop to hold her daughter's hands. "Jessie, there's more to college than sororities and trying to fit in, maybe you just need t- . . ." Jessie interjects, "Mom, this isn't even just the sororities. **It feels like a lot of organizations aspire to have the same type of selectivity as sororities and fraternities which I think doesn't make any sense because a sorority is completely different from, like, an international student organization. The Divine Nine can do their own thing, because that's them and that's their history and all, but I feel like we don't need that everywhere. Like . . . why try to replicate something that you don't need to replicate?"**

"It'll get better JJ, I promise, do you want some dessert?" Her mom looks into her eyes, not sure what else to say, she didn't go to college, she never lived in a residence hall, and definitely hadn't had this struggle.

November 28, 2022

Dear Diary,

I feel like being home for break really helped me understand and name some of the feelings I had been having this semester. Most of my friends felt the same way, you know, wanting to be involved but just not knowing how to get involved. We all made a promise that we would try to get involved more intentionally before we leave for winter break and not let these elitist barriers get in our way. It's weird because being in the mix is something we all missed so much from when we were all online, it felt like we were almost in a fish tank, **you see all these you see these people you want to meet, that you want to build these connections with and the people on the other side, they want to build those connections with you, they want to grow their organization and their club and get to know you, but that was ultimate disconnect,** we were virtual, but now we're in person. So diary, stay tuned! Let's get involved.

"Jessie, can I speak to you after class?" Dr. Larker, Jessie's first-year experience course professor asked her before she packed her bag up after class. "Yeah, of course Dr. Larker." Jessie walks up to her desk in the front of the classroom and asks, "what's up?" Dr. Larker looks at her and asks if she has class or anywhere she needs to be after this, Jessie nods her head no, this is her last class on Mondays. Dr. Larker says, "Perfect, come with me" and they walk back to her office. Dr. Larker gestures for Jessie to have a seat in a comfy leather chair adjacent from her desk. "So, how's your first semester at MAU treating you?" Jessie fakes a smile and responds, "It's going . . . you know, I am still getting adjusted, but it's good." Jessie had never gone to Dr. Larker's office hours, her eyes scan her office and bookshelves that are decorated with paraphernalia from her sorority, beautiful faux yellow roses, pearls falling from a Greek letter statue, her stole from graduation, pictures of her and her sorority sisters from the early 2000s and books on sisterhood, college experience and the excellence of Black women and her doctoral regalia hanging in the corner.

Dr. Larker looks at Jessie and thinks to herself, taking time to get adjusted to campus life is a Mid-Atlantic tale as old as time, "what's giving you trouble with getting adjusted?" Jessie slowly takes her eyes off the bookshelf and comes back to reality, "Huh? Oh, I just have been having trouble getting involved and how you say in class, finding my tribe. **I feel like, to get involved, they say it's easy, but it's so many steps that a person has to go through. A lot of information is spread through word of mouth and it's one of those things that if you know, you know and if you don't you miss out.** And sometimes, even when I know, I don't have the money for it or tickets sell out before I can get there." Dr. Larker reassures Jessie that she is not the first or last student to feel this way and it's a shame that some student's experience this every year. "Coming to such a selective institution can be a huge culture shock, **even at a place like an HBCU where we all have this common trait of identifying with Blackness or coming to this HBCU, and so off rip, I think that identity is something that brings people together. But that doesn't mean that it isn't hard for everyone to be communal.** In this area, it can be very competitive, a game of who's who, if you will. It's a very different experience than I had at my small, rural HBCU, I feel for you." Jessie takes a sigh of relief and thinks to herself, okay so I'm not crazy, "It's definitely harder here or at least it feels like . . ." Jessie's phone starts going off incessantly "Sorry Dr. Larker." She glances at her phone to silence it but sees the notifications and her face lights up with excitement but within seconds, like a balloon deflating, she settles into a disappointed slump.

Dr. Larker asks, "What just happened there?" Jessies adjusts her posture and straightens up to talk to Dr. Larker, "My roommate just sent me the flyer for this event you have to attend if you want to participate in membership intake for any of the Greek organizations and it's tomorrow night . . . but it's also $30 and I don't get paid until Friday, I don't even have anything appropriate to wear, it says business attire required." Dr. Larker smiles and begins to reach into her desk's lower drawer, "Well, that's just something you can't miss out on!" Jessie sighs, "But how can I go if I don't even have anything to wear, even if I do find $30 . . ." Dr. Larker interrupts, "I've seen your outfits every Monday for the last 12 weeks, you have an outfit. Be sure to wear that black blazer, white blouse, and black slacks you've worn, put them all together and you'll be fine! As for the cost of attending, take this," Dr. Larker takes Jessie's hand and puts cash into her hand, "and be the shining student and woman I know you are. I don't want to hear any excuses. Getting involved and finding your tribe will only get more challenging as time goes on. I have upperclassmen who had to move off campus, nearly 30 minutes away and they say they have nowhere to go in between class and events, so they just leave. No excuses, okay?" Jessie could barely find the words except thank you so much and oh my gosh in return for this gesture from her professor, who she had only known for a few months at this point.

November 30, 2022

Dear Diary,
Tonight is the prerequisite event for membership intake in the spring for all of the fraternities and sororities and me and Meech are going! Dr. Larker gave me the money for the registration fee and we were able to grab a few of the last spots to register!! They were not lying when they say that HBCUs are just different, our professors really, **genuinely are there for us in a way to build us up and empower us so that when you go out into the wider world, you're ready.** She really did not have to do that, I hope I can get picked and make her proud. I'm so excited, but I still can't shake the feeling that I am stepping into the most selective and elitism ridden room I've ever found myself in. I hope that I can get picked, get involved in more organizations and clubs and create more inclusive places for all MAU students. **My ideal situation would be where there's minimal elitism and selectivity in things that don't need to be selective, and then a nice**

balance of academics, but also just good old college years fun. Experiences where it's just catered towards college students just having a good time, something that's not related to campus, or organizations and stuff, just fun.

What Did We Learn from Jessie?

In the words of one of our participants,

> Legacy kids . . . they kind of put people under them in certain student leadership roles and/or organizations. And it is definitely not out of malice, if I really had someone coming up in my HBCU and I had the resources to get them into the space that they're interested in then I might do that but what that does on the foot end . . . for people who aren't as connected on campus, it may end up kicking them out of a space that they might be more qualified for or they might be more passionate about and it creates an inequity in regards to who is allowed in certain organizations."

As reflected in Jessie's experience, most of our participants agreed that elitism was prevalent on campus, going beyond a group of cliquey students or legacy students, but embedded into the culture of MAU. This elitism, too, permeates beyond the Black Greek Letter Organizations (BGLOs), leading students to feel disconnected from others. We also found that campus leaders can address students' disconnect by bringing up elitism and how it impacts students. By providing support, connectedness, mattering, value, respect, and importance (Strayhorn, 2012), HBCU professionals can uplift students who feel left on the outskirts by remembering that the full college experience goes beyond academic affairs and checking in with students to see how they are adjusting to their new campuses and environment.

Furthermore, as underscored by studies such as Winkle-Wagner and McCoy (2018), HBCU faculty can play a pivotal role in filling inclusion gaps for students, especially by allowing students to see themselves represented and cared for when their fields of study may not be as racially diverse.

As staff and faculty ensure that their students are successful and achieve sense of belonging, it is important to remove as many barriers as possible—small or big—for students to take full advantage of their HBCU experience. As reflected in Jessie's story, barriers such as student organization fees, on top of the pressures that students feel to fit in can be detrimental to experiencing sense of belonging. As student affairs staff plan campus events, it is important to provide ample time for students to plan ahead financially, as well as to leverage student fees and other operational budgets to lessen additional financial burden to students.

For many students, HBCUs are the first places in their academic journey where students can feel accepted and embraced (J. L. Williams et al., 2021). As highlighted by Jessie's story, the college experience can be daunting because of the financial stress of paying for college. Because HBCUs have excelled at supporting students deemed unready by other schools, we push HBCU leaders and educators to set the example for how Black students, regardless of socioeconomic background, can find themselves thriving through rich and inclusive campus involvement.

Given that social class can be visible (Bettencourt, 2021), it can create social class hierarchies on campus, as exemplified by Jessie and her roommate Meech when spotting the "perfect" legacy student on the yard. It is important to remove such barriers on campus to help close socioeconomic status gaps faced by students using effective interventions. Some of these interventions may include without limits: campus food pantries, business professional career clothing closets, interest meetings for campus organizations, and other career development resources. Furthermore, we urge HBCU leaders to advocate for more on campus housing options for students at all academic levels, as well as more affordable off-campus housing options to encourage a true sense of belonging even if they cannot live on campus.

Lastly, student interactions with faculty are integral to their HBCU experience. Just as Jessie experienced, another student in our research study stated,

> I transferred in with college credits from a community college because I was a dual enrollment student. And although my community college teachers while I was in high school really, really cared about us and wanted us to get that work done, it's just nothing like the love of a HBCU professor who really wants to see you do well not only in the class but outside of the class as well.

HBCUs are often characterized as familial environments where Black students feel supported instead of marginalized (J. L. Williams et al., 2021). Many faculty do not know of the impact they are having on students outside of the classroom. We want faculty to feel empowered that their interactions with students inside and outside of the classroom go beyond preparing them for life after college. Faculty can create moments of tangible feelings of support, connectedness, mattering, value, respect, and importance. In other words, a true sense of belonging for which HBCU students yearn for. (Strayhorn, 2012).

Appendix

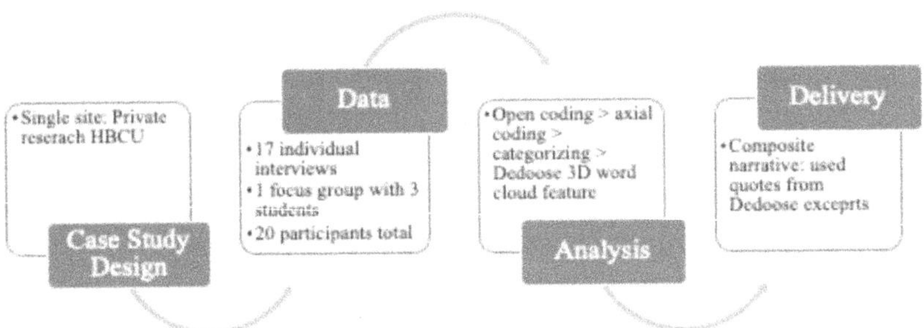

Figure 4.1 Methodology process. Author made.

Acknowledgments: We give credit to Natalie Muñoz, Walter Servance, and Marisa Thornton for their data collection and analysis efforts. We give thanks to the NACA Foundation for funding this study "They Just So Happen to be Born in the Right Family": A Story of Elitism on an HBCU Campus.

References

Bettencourt, G. M. (2021). "I belong because it wasn't made for me": Understanding working-class students' sense of belonging on campus. *The Journal of Higher Education*, *92*(5), 760–783.

Burmicky, J., Rzucidlo, K., Muñoz, N., Servance, W., & Thornton, M. (2022). Mattering and belonging: An HBCU case study exploration of campus involvement during the pandemic. *The Journal of Negro Education, 91*(3), 309-321. https://www.muse.jhu.edu/article/901989.

Cook, D. A. (2013). Blurring the boundaries: The mechanics of creating composite characters. In Marvin Lynn, Adrienne D. Dixson (Eds.), *Handbook of critical race theory in education* (pp. 201–214). Routledge.

Green, E. L. (2022, June 11). Why students are choosing HBCUs: "4 years being seen as family." *The New York Times*. https://www.nytimes.com/2022/06/11/us/hbcu-enrollment-black-students.html

Harris, A. (2021). *The state must provide: Why America's colleges and universities have always been unequal—and how to set them right.* HarperCollins.

Howard-Woods, C., Laidley, C., & Omidi, M. (2019). *#Charlottesville: White supremacy, populism, and resistance* (Howard-Woods, C. Laidley, & M. Omidi, Eds.). Public Seminar Books in association with OR Books.

Miles, M., Huberman, A., & Saldaña, J. (2014). *Qualitative data analysis: A methods sourcebook* (3rd ed.). Sage.

Miller, G. N., Lynn, F. B., & McCloud, L. I. (2021). By lack of reciprocity: Positioning historically Black colleges and universities in the organizational field of higher education. *The Journal of Higher Education, 92*(2), 194–226. https://www.tandfonline.com/doi/full/10.1080/00221546.2020.1803026

Palmer, R. T., & Maramba, D. C. (2015). Racial microaggressions among Asian American and Latino/a students at a historically Black university. *Journal of College Student Development, 56*, 705–722. https://doi.org/10.1353/csd.2015.0076

Palmer, R. T., & Williams, J. L. (2021). "Peeling back the layers": A deeper look at the diversity among Black students at historically Black colleges and universities. *Journal of Diversity in Higher Education*. https://doi.org/10.1037/dhe0000358

Saldaña, J. (2011). *Fundamentals of qualitative research*. Oxford university press

Smith, S. A. (2015). *On and* off *the* stage *at Atlanta Greek Picnic: Performances of* collective black middle-class identities *and the* politics *of belonging* Doctoral dissertation, Florida International University, *SCISPACE. https://scispace.com/pdf/on-and-off-the-stage-at-atlanta-greek-picnic-performances-of-1x6l5nivc5.pdf*

Stake, R. E. (2008). Qualitative case studies. In N. K. Denzin & Y. S. Lincoln (Eds.), *Strategies of qualitative inquiry* (pp. 119–149). Sage

Strayhorn, T. L. (2012). *College students' sense of belonging: A key to educational success for all students*. Routledge.

Strayhorn, T. L. (2019). Sense of belonging and student success at historically black colleges and universities: A key to strategic enrollment management and institutional transformation. In F. L. Bonner, A. F. Lomotey, & P. A. Howard (Eds.), Examining student retention and engagement strategies at historically Black colleges and universities (pp. 32–52). IGI Global.

Strayhorn, T. L. (2021). Analyzing the short-term impact of a brief web-based intervention on first-year students' sense of belonging at an HBCU: A quasi-experimental study. *Innovative Higher Education*. https://doi.org/10.1007/s10755-021-09559-5

Strayhorn, T. L. (2022). Analyzing national databases in student affairs assessment at historically Black colleges and universities (HBCUs). *New Directions for Student Services, 2022*(178–179), 163–174. https://doi.org/10.1002/ss.20437

Strayhorn, T. L. (2023). Analyzing the short-term impact of a brief web-based intervention on first-year students' sense of belonging at an HBCU: A quasi-experimental study. *Innovative Higher Education*, *48*, 1–13. https://doi.org/10.1007/s10755-021-09559-5

Strayhorn, T. L., & Terrell, M. C. (2010). *The evolving challenges of Black college students: New insights for policy, practice, and research*. Stylus.

Taylor, B. (2008). Color and class: The promulgation of elitist attitudes at Black colleges. In M. Gasman & C. L. Tudico (Eds.), Historically Black colleges and universities (pp. 189–206). Palgrave Macmillan.

Williams, K. L., Burt, B. A., Clay, K. L., & Bridges, B. K. (2019). Stories untold: counter-narratives to anti-blackness and deficit-oriented discourse concerning HBCUs. *American Educational Research Journal, 56*(2), 556–599. https://doi.org/10.3102/0002831218802776

Williams, K. L., Russell, A., & Summerville, K. (2021). Centering blackness: An examination of culturally-affirming pedagogy and practices enacted by HBCU administrators and faculty members. *Innovative Higher Education*, *46*, 733–757. https://doi.org/10.1007/s10755-021-09562-w

Williams, J. L., Palmer, R. T., & Jones, B. J. (2021). "Where I can breathe": Examining the impact of the current racial climate on Black students' choice to attend historically Black colleges and universities. *Journal of Black Studies, 52*(8), 795–819. https://doi.org/10.1177/00219347211039833

Willis, R. (2019). The use of composite narratives to present interview findings. *Qualitative Research, 19*(4), 471–480.

Winkle-Wagner, R., & McCoy, D. L. (2018). Feeling like an "Alien" or "Family"? Comparing students and faculty experiences of diversity in STEM disciplines at a PWI and an HBCU. *Race, Ethnicity and Education, 21*(5), 593–606. https://doi.org/10.1080/13613324.2016.1248835

Yin, R. K. (2009). *Case study research: Design and methods* (5h ed.). Sage.

5

Toward Beloved Communities on Campus

Understanding the Intersections of Race, Gender, and Sexual Identity in Sense of Belonging Research as a Tool for Rethinking Campus Resources

Erik Malewski, Genevieve Weber, Christina Turner, and Katrina Alford

Chapter Outline

The larger your beloved community, the more you can accomplish in the world.

—Thich Nhat Hanh

Beloved community is formed not by the eradication of difference but by its affirmation, by each of us claiming the identities and cultural legacies that shape who we are and how we live in the world.

—bell hooks

Introduction

Undergraduate student populations continue to diversify around social identities that include race, gender, sexual identity, and intersections of these identities (Irwin et al., 2022). As student diversity increases and new meaning is made from single- and intersectional identities, higher education researchers aspire to better understand how students make sense of their campus experiences with particular attention to differential perceptions based on unique social locations. Bejarano and Valverde (2012) noted inadequate ways that universities work on "acculturation to sameness" through programs that remove students from family and community contexts and integrate them into campus life. This chapter challenges such assimilation efforts and upholds the belief that different student groups respond differently to campus environments and their experiences should be viewed through varied and unique lenses. How students perceive and experience their campus climate shapes key student outcomes that include, but are not limited to, retention, progression, critical thinking, and cultural knowledge (Hurtado et al., 2012; Rankin & Reason, 2008; Tsui, 2000). A key measure of student responses to campus environments is sense of belonging (Strayhorn, 2019). Strayhorn described sense of belonging as "a basic human need" and refers to students' perceptions of "social support," feelings related to "connectedness," and experiences that give evidence of "mattering" and "feeling cared for" by campus community members as core conditions to this measure (p. 4).

Sense of belonging researchers have found that minoritized undergraduate students experience higher education differently from their majority peers (Strayhorn, 2019; Vaccaro & Newman, 2016) Variations in sense of belonging have been found along race (Duran et al., 2020; Rainey et al., 2018), gender (Master & Meltzoff, 2020), and sexual identity (Vaccaro & Newman, 2017) and noted to impact persistence (Gopalan & Brady, 2020). This chapter highlights how colleges and universities have been unsuccessful at developing campus climates that engender a sense of belonging for students with one minoritized identity marker, which is only compounded by multiple minoritized identity markers. While understanding race, gender, and sexual identity separately is insightful, it is increasingly insufficient as it does not address the dynamic needs of undergraduate students who face unique stressors associated with intersecting identities and what that means for sense of belonging and whether they stay at their institution.

Using data from Rankin Climate's[1] database with over 200 colleges and universities, we examined sense of belonging and departure intentions (e.g., whether respondents contemplated leaving their institution) for different racial, gender, and sexual identity groups and their intersections. This study aligns with other intersectionality research that examines the crossroads of different identity markers, resulting in forms of experience and oppression unique to particular standpoints (e.g., Duran et al., 2020; Valdez & Golash-Boza, 2020). Accordingly, we investigated how institutional climates shaped students' experiences differently based on one or multiple minoritized identity markers. This analysis was guided by the following questions:

---

[1]Rankin Climate is a North American consulting firm that conducts climate research for colleges and universities. See rankinclimate.com for more information.

(Q1) How does undergraduate student sense of belonging differ by student race, gender identity, and sexual identity?

(Q2) How do student intersectional identities (e.g., race and gender, gender and sexual identity, and race and sexual identity) impact student sense of belonging?

(Q3) How do students with intersectional identities, that have higher or lower reported sense of belonging, differ from their peers when evaluating if they have seriously considered leaving their institutions?

Our research findings underscore more meaningful ways to conceptualize and prioritize campus resources. Given the growing attention to sense of belonging and its relationship to retention, progression, and overall student success (O'Keeffe, 2013), we call to action administrators, faculty, and staff to envision new approaches to student support. To do so, we must be open and willing to understand a more complicated picture of our basic human need to feel valued, cared for, and that we belong. On college and university campuses, this translates to all students feeling that their voices, presence, and contributions matter, grounded in the identities they hold.

Positionality Statements

Informed by feminist standpoint theory, we were motivated to describe our backgrounds as a way of understanding how we approached data analysis and corresponding results and discussion. Feminist standpoint theory highlights the importance of scholars delineating how their viewpoints, subject positions, and worldviews informed research processes and interpretations of data (Lather, 1992; Naples & Gurr, 2013). Erik Malewski identifies as a white queer scholar from a working-class background who is interested in discourse analysis, post-structural ideas, and the ways that language reveals connection and alienation within educational settings. Genevieve Weber is a white, cisgender woman, and first-generation scholar who is focused on counseling and mental health with a lifelong commitment to social justice for minoritized people. Katrina Alford is a Latina doctoral candidate in rural sociology and demography with a focus on quantitative methodologies, community development, and equity issues in rural settings. Christina Turner is a white, queer, disabled researcher interested in institutional betrayal, pastoral care, and ideal worker norms in higher education. These positionalities informed our methods, analysis, results, and discussion, with a focus on race, gender, and sexual identity, as we advance sense of belonging and campus resource literatures.

Literature Review

Intersectionality

While the concept of intersectionality has entered broader public discourse as a part of manufactured political controversies over critical race theory in education, the idea of intersectionality is typically associated with Kimberly Crenshaw's (1989) work in critical legal theory. Crenshaw builds upon historical Black feminist intellectual thought to help explain that Black women, by the way race and gender are inextricably bound together, end up erased by the systemic forces of racial and gender oppression. In a society structured around single identity politics (in this chapter, single identity markers), Black women could not find a home in civil rights movements predicated on the needs and leadership of Black men and leadership or feminist movements built around the needs and leadership of white women. While initially framed around legal doctrine that advanced racial and gender equality separately and the ways that Black women are lost in such a binary, intersectionality has since been used as a theoretical tool to explain how various overlapping identities result in unique experiences that cannot be unbound from each other, inform each other, and often result in the complex convergence of different forms of oppression.

With regards to sense of belonging, the same phenomenon—a focus on a single identity marker—has been at play until recently. Sense of belonging has focused on race (Duran et al., 2020; Rainey et al., 2018), gender (Master & Meltzoff, 2020), and sexual identity (Vaccaro & Newman, 2017). While such research has been of significant benefit to deepening knowledge of belonging, in particular how various groups perceive and experience fitting in, the lack of intersectional analysis in such research might mean it masked as much as it revealed. For example, prior research has offered some examination of transpectrum[2] students' sense of belonging but little research on how racial minoritization intersects with transpectrum identities toward better informed, and particularized, frameworks for sense of belonging. Intersectionality provides an opportunity to develop more complex pictures of how interwoven prejudices shape experiences and perceptions at the crossroads of various identity markers toward more "complicated conversations" (Pinar, 2019) regarding sense of belonging. In the remainder of this literature review, we examine single identity marker research with the recognition that the next step to advance sense of belonging involves intersecting identity markers and, in the case of this chapter, the implications for campus resources.

Race and Undergraduates

Black/African American

Studies illustrate the important roles that campus climate and racial representation play in sense of belonging for Black/African American undergraduates. Black men at predominantly white institutions (PWI) have a lower sense of belonging than their peers at Historically Black Colleges and Universities (HBCUs) (Strayhorn et al., 2015). Numerous studies illustrate that Black students experience overt and covert racism at PWIs that results in a lower sense of belonging (Harper & Hurtado, 2007; Johnson, 2012). Duran et al. (2020) found that for both first-generation and continuing-generation African American undergraduates, experiences with racism had a significant negative effect on their sense of belonging. Lewis et al. (2021), in a mixed-methods study, found that African American students experienced a greater frequency of racial microaggressions than other racial and ethnic minorities, including those who identified as multiracial. Studies with Black undergraduates who

---

[2]Authors use "transpectrum" as an umbrella term to describe the gender identity of individuals who do not identify as cisgender. Identities may include transgender, gender non-binary, genderqueer, and/or agender, in addition to other non-cisgender identities.

hold intersectional marginalized identities highlight a compounding effect of marginalization for this population that results in a lower sense of belonging (Strayhorn, 2019).

The literature offers numerous experiences and services that increase a sense of belonging in Black undergraduates. Strayhorn et al. (2015) has noted that same-race peer interactions seem to function as a protective factor that sustains a sense of belonging. Similarly, participation in Black cultural centers (Patton, 2006) and racial identity focused clubs and organizations (Harper & Quaye, 2007) seem to have a similar sustaining effect on a sense of belonging for Black undergraduate students. Interactions with faculty and staff that are affirming and humanizing can also increase Black students' sense of belonging (Johnson, 2019; Newman et al., 2015; Strayhorn, 2008). Brooms (2020) found that positive faculty interactions, faculty behaviors of associated care, and faculty mentorship all increased Black men's sense of belonging and success. Positive, validating messages from faculty members and increased interactions with faculty members in and out of the classroom also were found to increase a sense of belonging for Black undergraduates (Newman et al., 2015).

Hispanic/Latin American [Latine]

It is documented in the literature that Latine undergraduates have a lower sense of belonging than white undergraduate students (Strayhorn, 2008; Núñez, 2009). The same research, however, suggests that common factors that increase sense of belonging for some groups might not be as impactful to Latine students. For example, living on campus might not help Latine students build community and a sense of belonging as it does for other groups (Strayhorn, 2008). Further, Núñez (2009) found that Latino students who report more academic and social connection also experience a greater sense of engagement and a more hostile campus climate. McGee (2016) and Hurtado and Ponjuan (2005) both noted that Latine responses to racial stereotyping have been denial of systemic barriers and reported disengagement from their cultural identities toward the dominant cultures, particularly when enrolled in white dominated academic majors. These unique and complex findings in regard to sense of belonging for Latine undergraduate students call for particular attention to how they engage and experience belonging.

For Latine college students, course grades, time spent on academic studies, and interactions with diverse peers impacted sense of belonging (Strayhorn, 2008). Multiple studies showed that positive quality interactions with diverse peers led to a higher sense of belonging and increased sense of confidence and skills for Latino students (Strayhorn, 2008; Johnson et al., 2007). Similarly, for Latinos, sense of belonging increased when these students had closer relationships with faculty and administrators at their institutions (García et al., 2016). Participation in academic support programs increased sense of belonging and confidence in analytical skills in Latine college students (Hurtado & Ponjuan, 2005). Inconsistent with Strayhorn (2008), Duran et al. (2020) noted that living on campus had a positive impact on the sense of belonging among continuing generation Latine students. The role of campus residential living in increased sense of belonging might be more salient for Latine students from families who have experienced higher education as it helps them follow the paths of their family members.

Asian American and Pacific Islander

There is a paucity of research on campus climate and sense of belonging for Asian American and Pacific Islander (AAPI) college students (Nguyen et al., 2016). Despite limited investigations, a sentiment that this group is thriving has prevailed, silencing the voices of those AAPI undergraduate students who might benefit from academic, social, or psychological support (Maramba & Museus, 2013). Studies by Museus and Truong (2009) and Maramba (2008) disaggregated data of AAPI college students and uncovered substantial within-group differences and a low sense of belonging for some subgroups within the overall AAPI data set. Findings by Nguyen et al. (2018) provided additional context to these findings by highlighting the microaggressions experienced by AAPI college students coupled with feelings of being "unrecognized, invisible, intolerant, disrespected, and unsupported" (p. 497), isolated, and disconnected. A less welcoming campus climate, according to Yi and Todd (2022), may lead to a lack a sense of belonging, one in which AAPI students conform or assimilate rather than challenge the majority culture on campus; this finding is similar to Latine findings referenced above on Latine responses to responses to racial stereotyping.

Research on improving sense of belonging for AAPI students is unique and complex in that it involves a number of interpersonal and intrapersonal factors (Slaten et al., 2016). Slaten's et al. qualitative study highlighted the role of academic achievement and academic success in the sense of belonging felt by AAPI college students. Finding peers who were similarly committed to academic achievement—whether from their same country of origin or domestic—was a primary goal for AAPI students, but not all peers served the same roles in creating campus connections (Slaten et al., 2016). More specific, peers who shared in nationality helped increase AAPI college students social support and sense of security (Slaten et al., 2016). Campus venues and facilities (e.g., ethnic organizations, multicultural centers, ethnic studies courses) that foster ethnic group cohesion were identified as supportive measures where AAPI students could explore their racial and ethnic backgrounds, strengthening their social self-efficacy. Higher social self-efficacy for AAPI students is associated with increased cross-cultural connections to others on campus (Maramba & Museus, 2013; Slaten et al., 2016). For international or first-generation AAPI students, interactions with peers who did not share in their nationality or culture were described by Slaten et al. as helping them increase their awareness of US social and cultural dynamics, further connecting them to the campus environment.

Gender and Undergraduates

Studies have consistently shown that white men undergraduates report the highest sense of belonging while women of color undergraduates report the lowest sense of belonging (Lewis et al., 2021; Rainey et al., 2018). In addition to university-wide studies, women, and transpectrum undergraduates also consistently report a lower sense of belonging within their disciplines, particularly science, technology, engineering, and math (Johnson, 2012; Mooney & Becker, 2020). Dortch and Patel (2017) found that lower sense of belonging for Black undergraduate women in STEM fields was related to an intersection of racial and gender discrimination and experiences of isolation, marginalization, and alienation, ones that often resulted from microaggressions. Similarly, Rodriguez and Blaney (2021) reported that Latina undergraduates who were in STEM majors often reported feeling marginalized and isolated, and described how their male peers were skeptical of their abilities, which resulted in experiences with self-doubt and self-depreciation. Dortch and Patel (2017) concluded that white men continue to benefit from the stereotype fit regarding who pursues and belongs in STEM fields while women must fight those stereotypes.

In order to increase sense of belonging, the literature offers a series of inclusive practices that increase women and gender minorities' sense of belonging. Dortch and Patel (2017) denote the importance of enrolling women and gender minorities in numbers significant enough that they can create their own communities and authentic relationships, as well as serve as peer role models. African American undergraduate women reported a higher sense of community and willingness to persist when faculty are approachable, accessible, excited about what they teach, and authentic in their instructional approaches and relationship building with students (Booker, 2016). Similarly, Johnson (2012) noted the importance of faculty awareness of the ways they shape campus climates around race and gender so as to create positive mentoring experiences. Within the STEM disciplines, Mooney and Becker (2020) found female computer science students who participated in networking, outreach, and mentoring activities also reported a higher sense of belonging. STEM students' sense of belonging was also found to correlate with the number of students with the same gender who were also in their major (Rainey et al., 2018). Master and Meltzoff (2020) found that teachings that broaden beliefs about STEM, encourage growth mindsets that lessen the impact of negative stereotypes, and normalize doubts about belonging create an increased sense of belonging for undergraduate women STEM majors. Similarly, Good et al. (2012) found that a growth mindset—where women undergraduates believed math knowledge could be acquired—resulted in a high sense of belonging and intention to continue in the field.

LGBTQ+/Queerspectrum and Transpectrum Undergraduates

The literature on queerspectrum and transpectrum college students suggests that straight and cisgender identified college students perceive their campuses as less hostile and more welcoming (Rankin et al., 2019). Positive perceptions of campus environments, including a sense of safety and support for self-expression, lead to an increased sense of belonging (Wilson & Liss, 2022; Gano, 2021; Parker, 2021; Vaccaro & Newman,

2017), and this includes queerspectrum students of color (Duran et al., 2020) and non-binary students (Budge et al., 2020). Unfortunately, the research literature reveals that both queerspectrum and transpectrum college students more frequently report that their campuses are hostile and that they experience physical and verbal abuse and microaggressions (Blackmon et al., 2020; Hughes & Hurtado, 2018; Tetreault et al., 2013). Queerspectrum and transpectrum college students have also reported that, when they experience hostile campus environments, they also feel increased isolation and disengagement from others from whom they might find community and support (Gano, 2021).

The literature on sense of belonging denotes that transpectrum college students experience belonging when they develop meaningful relationships, particularly authentic relationships with individuals who hold similar identities (Duran, 2019; Gano, 2021; Gonyo, 2016; Vaccaro & Newman, 2017). These authentic relationships are characterized by comfort in sharing one's whole self without judgment, freedom of expression without censorship, and overall validation and support (Duran, 2019; Gano, 2021; Vaccaro & Newman, 2017). Similar to authentic relationships, the literature also suggests some curricular experiences help build a sense of belonging among queerspectrum and transpectrum college students. Duran et al. (2020) found a positive correlation between the frequency of interactions with faculty and an increased sense of belonging for queerspectrum students of color. Gano (2021) reported findings that highlight the roles of systematic academic study, academic success, and participation in faculty-led research projects in increasing sense of belonging for queerspectrum and transpectrum college students. Gonyo (2016) found similar findings in a study of Black gay men at predominantly white institutions. Vaccaro and Newman (2017) reported that queerspectrum and transpectrum college students found community, resources, and support in resource centers.

Research Design

Using the large, multi-institution dataset, our research team hoped to assess the relationships between student identities (e.g., race, gender identity, and sexual identity), sense of belonging, and *if students have ever seriously considered leaving* their institutions, using language from the original survey. We engaged in a three-step process for developing our research questions and analyzing our data, guided by the results produced in the previous step.

We first set out to assess Q1. After initial findings highlighted specific identities that were associated with generally higher or lower student sense of belonging, our team questioned the role that intersectionality played in sense of belonging outcomes. We then went back to the data to understand Q2. Our second step of the research process led us to identify four intersectional identity groups—two with the highest and two with the lowest reported sense of belonging. Knowing that student sense of belonging is correlated with intent to persist (Gopalan & Brady, 2020), we were led to our final research question, Q3.

Sample/Participants/Instrument

Data for this study were drawn from the *Assessment of Climate for Learning, Living, and Working*, a survey designed to assess campus climate for students, staff, and faculty administered at over 200 institutions in North America. For the research that follows, we organized data from surveys that were administered between 2016 and 2022 at 33 public and 16 private 4-year institutions in the United States and Canada, where data were collected from 74,889 undergraduate students. The 49 institutions varied in geographic location (e.g., West, South, Midwest, Northeast), community setting (e.g., remote town to large city), and Carnegie basic classification (e.g., doctoral universities to baccalaureate/associate colleges).

The survey comprised over 100 questions and presented respondents the opportunity to provide information about their personal campus experiences, their perceptions of the campus climate, and their perceptions of institutional actions; one section elicited demographic information such as race and gender. Institutions customized some response options to their institutional context and population, including response options for social

Table 5.1 Sample Statistics

	Percent (*Mean*)	N
Student Sense of Belonging	*(3.81)*	**74,889**
Seriously Considered Leaving		**72,212**
Yes	28.9	20,873
No	71.1	51,339
Race		**70,919**
White	67.5	47,860
Asian/Pacific Islander	9.2	6,541
Black	6.0	4,225
Latine	7.5	5,329
Multiracial	9.8	6,964
Gender		**72,956**
Transpectrum	2.0	1,489
Men	33.2	24,227
Women	64.8	47,240
Sexual Identity		**70,009**
Heterosexual	85.1	59,609
LGBQ	14.9	10,400

Note: All students included in this study answered the questions necessary to calculate a sense of belonging score. However, all other questions in the survey were optional. Because of this, the sum of the race, gender, and sexual identity categories will not equal 74,889.

identities. To run analyses, certain responses were combined to make comparisons between groups and ensure respondents' confidentiality; as an example, racial and ethnic identity response choices were collapsed into five categories: white, Asian American Pacific Islander, Black, Latine, and multiracial. See Table 5.1 for respondent demographic information.

Data Collection and Measures

The dependent variables used in this analysis were two outcome variables: a nine-item factor regarding students' sense of belonging and a dichotomous variable as to whether students ever seriously considered leaving the institution. The sense of belonging scale was informed by Strayhorn's (2019) qualitative examination of students' sense of belonging. Rankin Climate developed survey questions to quantitatively measure sense of belonging for students. Respondents ranked their level of agreement from 1 (strongly disagree) to 5 (strongly agree) with statements such as "I feel valued by [institution name] senior administrators" and "I have faculty whom I perceive as role models." The dependent variable in Chi-square analyses was measured by an item that asked "Have you ever seriously considered leaving [institution]?" and response options were 1 (yes) and 0 (no). Independent variables were respondents' self-reported identity markers: race (white, AAPI, Black, Latine, multiracial), gender (transpectrum, man, woman), and sexual identity (queerspectrum or heterosexual).

Quality and Accuracy of Data

Reliability and validity measures established trustworthiness. Reliability was established via evaluation of instrument structure to ensure stability, consistent responses, and consistent administration. Expected a posteriori (EAP) scoring provided a measure of the sense of belonging scale's high internal consistency reliability, which suggested the scale produced consistent results. Evidence for validity of interpretations was established by development of survey items and subject matter expert review. Items and response options arose from literature review of campus climate studies, twenty years of prior instrument development and survey administrations, and input from campus community members.

Analysis

To address our research questions, we utilized group-mean comparison testing, including both ANOVA and Chi-squared (X^2) tests. We used ANOVA to establish significant differences in student sense of belonging by both single identity markers and multiple identity markers (see Table 5.2). First, we compared significant differences by race (e.g., white vs. Black; Latine vs. multiracial), gender (e.g., transpectrum vs. men; women vs. men), and sexual identity (e.g., heterosexual vs. queerspectrum). Then, we also used ANOVA to assess how multiple identity markers impact sense of belonging scores. We compared mean sense of belonging score differences between racial groups by gender (e.g., white transpectrum vs. minority

Table 5.2 Average Sense of Belonging by Single Identity Markers

	N	Mean (SD)	95% Confidence Interval Lower	95% Confidence Interval Upper
Total	74,889	3.81 (0.72)	–	–
Race				
White	47,860	3.86 (0.70)	3.85	3.87
Asian/Pacific Islander	6,541	3.77 (0.70)	3.76	3.79
Black	4,225	3.63 (0.76)	3.61	3.66
Latine	5,329	3.78 (0.75)	3.76	3.80
Multiracial	6,964	3.73 (0.72)	3.71	3.75
Gender				
Transpectrum	1,489	3.53 (0.76)	3.49	3.57
Men	24,227	3.80 (0.74)	3.79	3.81
Women	47,240	3.83 (0.70)	3.83	3.84
Sexual Identity				
Heterosexual	59,609	3.84 (.71)	3.83	3.84
LGBQ	10,400	3.70 (0.71)	3.69	3.71

Note: Sense of Belonging was determined via factor analysis, with a minimum score of 1 and a maximum of 5. See "Data Collection" for more information on the Sense of Belonging Factor Analysis.

transpectrum; white women vs. AAPI women), sexual identity groups by gender (Heterosexual men vs. Queerspectrum men), and sexual identity groups by race (Heterosexual multiracial vs. Queerspectrum multiracial). We utilized Chi-square testing to compare those who had seriously considered leaving and those who had not, specifically identifying multiple identity marker groups that had either significantly high or significantly low sense of belonging and comparing them to their peers. Last, we reviewed the reasons students provided as to why they seriously considered leaving, focused on those who had the lowest reported sense of belonging.

Results

Question 1

Among all undergraduate students in our sample ($n = 74{,}889$), the average sense of belonging score was 3.81 on a factor scale of 5.0 (see Table 5.3). With this, we saw variations and significant differences by student race, gender, and sexual identity (see Table 5.4).

Table 5.3 Average Sense of Belonging by Multiple Identity Markers

	Transpectrum		Man		Woman		Heterosexual		Queerspectrum	
	N	**Mean (SD)**	**N**	**Mean (SD)**	**N**	**Mean (SD)**	**N**	**Mean (SD)**	**N**	**Mean (SD)**
White	855	3.59 (0.73)	15,762	3.82 (0.73)	31,053	3.89 (0.68)	39,916	3.88 (0.70)	6,158	3.74 (0.68)
AAPI	141	3.55 (0.73)	2,417	3.82 (0.73)	3,945	3.75 (0.69)	5,098	3.78 (0.70)	1,023	3.69 (0.71)
Black	50	3.38 (0.86)	1,243	3.73 (0.74)	2,912	3.59 (0.75)	3,426	3.65 (0.75)	557	3.51 (0.76)
Latine	110	3.56 (0.82)	1,718	3.80 (0.75)	3,473	3.77 (0.74)	4,155	3.79 (0.74)	890	3.66 (3.66)
Multiracial	242	3.41 (0.80)	2,155	3.71 (0.76)	4,508	3.76 (0.69)	5,264	3.76 (0.71)	1,416	3.65 (0.71)
Heterosexual	243	3.59 (0.90)	20,657	3.81 (0.74)	38,566	3.86 (0.70)		-		-
Queerspectrum	965	3.55 (0.73)	2,611	3.76 (0.75)	6,702	3.70 (0.70)		-		-

Table 5.4 Mean Difference in Sense of Belonging by Multiple Identity Markers

			95% CI	
	Mean Difference	**SE**	**Lower**	**Upper**
Race and Gender				
Transpectrum				
White x Minority	0.13***	.01	0.12	0.15
Men				
White x AAPI	0.004	0.02	−0.04	0.05
White x Black	0.09***	0.02	0.03	0.15
White x Latine	0.02	0.02	−0.03	0.07
White x Multiracial	0.11***	0.02	0.06	0.16
AAPI x Black	0.09**	0.03	0.01	0.16
AAPI x Latine	0.02	0.02	−0.05	0.08
AAPI x Multiracial	0.11***	0.02	0.05	0.17
Black x. Latine	−0.07	0.03	−0.15	0.01
Black x Multiracial	0.02	0.03	−0.05	0.09
Latine x Multiracial	0.09**	0.02	0.02	0.16
Women				
White x AAPI	0.14***	0.01	0.10	0.17
White x Black	0.29***	0.01	0.26	0.33
White x Latine	0.12***	0.01	0.08	0.15
White x Multiracial	0.13***	0.01	0.10	0.16
AAPI x Black	0.16***	0.01	0.11	0.21
AAPI x Latine	−0.02	0.02	−0.06	0.03
AAPI x Multiracial	−0.01	0.02	−0.05	0.03
Black x. Latine	−0.18***	0.02	−0.23	−0.13
Black x Multiracial	−0.17***	0.02	−0.21	−0.12
Latine x Multiracial	0.01	0.02	−0.03	0.06
Gender and Sexual Identity				
Transpectrum				
Heterosexual x Queerspectrum	0.06	0.06	−0.07	0.18
Men				
Heterosexual x Queerspectrum	0.05**	0.02	0.02	0.08
Women				
Heterosexual x Queerspectrum	0.15***	0.01	0.14	0.17

(*Continued*)

Table 5.4 (Continued)

			95% CI	
	Mean Difference	**SE**	**Lower**	**Upper**
Race and Sexual Identity				
White				
Heterosexual x Queerspectrum	0.14***	.01	0.12	0.16
AAAPI				
Heterosexual x Queerspectrum	0.09***	0.2	0.04	0.14
Black				
Heterosexual x Queerspectrum	0.13***	0.03	0.06	0.20
Latine				
Heterosexual x Queerspectrum	0.13***	0.03	0.07	0.18
Multiracial				
Heterosexual x Queerspectrum	0.11***	0.02	0.07	0.15

Race. When looking at undergraduate students by race, white students (n = 47n,860) have the highest average reported sense of belonging (3.86). This is significantly higher than their peers of all other races: AAPI (n = 6,541, 3.8, $p < .001$), Black (n = 4,225, 3.6, $p < .001$), Latine (n = 5,329, 3.8, $p < .001$), and multiracial (n = 6,964, 3.7, $p < .001$). Black students have the lowest average reported sense of belonging, where it is significantly lower than their white ($p < .001$), AAPI ($p < .001$), Latine ($p < .001$), and multiracial ($p < .001$) peers.

Gender. Of gender identities, transpectrum students (n = 1n,489) reported the lowest sense of belonging (3.5). This is significantly lower than their peers who are men (n = 24,227, 3.8, $p < .001$) and women (n = 47,240, 3.8, $p < .001$). Additionally, men students' sense of belonging was significantly lower than women's ($p < .001$).

Sexual Identity. Among student sexual identities, queerspectrum students (n = 10,400) reported an average sense of belonging of 3.7, which is significantly lower than their heterosexual peers (n = 59,609, 3.8, $p < .001$).

Question 2

The findings above note that there are numerous multiple identity markers with significantly higher or lower reported sense of belonging among undergraduate students. Interested in how intersectionality may impact sense of belonging scores, we also compared mean scores by multiple identity markers—race and gender, gender and sexual identity, and race and sexual identity.

Race and Gender. Black transpectrum students (n = 50) have the lowest reported sense of belonging (3.4) among all other gender and race intersectional identity groups. For transpectrum students, n values were too small to draw any meaningful differences between individual racial groups; however, when comparing white transpectrum students (n = 855n) to their racially minoritized transpectrum peers (n = 543p), average sense of belonging is significantly higher (p < .001n) among white transpectrum students (3.6) than racially minoritized transpectrum students (3.5). Looking to men, white men undergraduate students (n = 15n,762) have significantly higher average sense of belonging (3.8) than their men peers who are Black (n = 1p,243, 3.7, p < .001n) and multiracial (n = 2p,155, 3.7, p < .001); however, white men's sense of belonging is not significantly different than AAPI or Latine men. Among all gender and race intersectional groups, white women (n = 31,053) have the highest average sense of belonging (3.9). This is significantly higher than their women peers who are AAPI (n =, 3.75, p < .001), Black (n =, 3.59, p < .001), Latine (n =, 3.8, p < .001), and multiracial (n =, 3.8, p < .0001p). Furthermore, among women students, Black women have the lowest reported sense of belonging (3.6); this is significantly lower than their peers of all other races (p < .001), while there are no significant differences between AAPI, Latine, and multiracial women.

Gender and Sexual Identity. For both queerspectrum men (n = 2n,611, 3.8) and queerspectrum women (= 6n,702, 3.7), their average reported sense of belonging is significantly lower than their heterosexual men (= 20p,657, 3.8, <.001n) and heterosexual women (n = 38p,566, 3.9, p < .001) peers, respectively. Among transpectrum students, no significant differences exist in reported sense of belonging between queerspectrum transpectrum students, and heterosexual transpectrum students. However, despite the lack of significant differences, it is noteworthy that queerspectrum, transpectrum students (n = 965) have the lowest average sense of belonging (3.5) of all gender and sexual multiple identity groups.

Race and Sexual Identity. As noted above, queerspectrum students report significantly lower sense of belonging than their heterosexual peers. This trend holds up regardless of race, where white queerspectrum (n = 6n,158, 3.7), AAPI queerspectrum (= 1n,023, 3.7), Black queerspectrum (= 557n, 3.5), Latine queerspectrum (= 890n, 3.7), and Multiracial queerspectrum (= 1p,416, 3.7) students all have significantly lower (< .001) sense of belonging than their heterosexual peers of the same race. Among the race and sexual identity multiple identity marker groups, Black queerspectrum students have the overall lowest reported average sense of belonging (3.5).

Question 3

The analysis addressing our second research question identified that white women and white heterosexual students have the highest average reported sense of belonging (3.89 and 3.88, respectively), whereas Black queerspectrum and racially minoritized transpectrum students have the lowest average reported sense of belonging (3.5 for both). With this information, the final research question addresses differences in intent to persist, comparing these four groups with their peers (see Table 5.5).

White Women. Of white women students (n = 30,364), just over one-quarter (26.5 percent, n = 8n,054) seriously considered leaving their institution. This is not significantly different than their white men peers (n = 15n,333), where 26.3 percent had seriously considered leaving. However, racially minoritized women (n = 13,987) seriously considered leaving at a significantly higher rate (33.9 percent) than their white women peers ($\chi 2$ = 251.1p, p < .001).

White Heterosexual. Roughly one-quarter (25.2 percent) of white heterosexual students (n = 38n,983) seriously considered leaving their institution. This is significantly lower than their peers who are white queerspectrum students (n = 6,026, 34.7 percent, $\chi 2$ = 240.4p, p < .001n) and minority heterosexual students (n = 16,923, 31.9 percent, $\chi 2$ = 261.5p, p < .001).

Black Queerspectrum. Nearly half (47.6 percent) of Black queerspectrum students (n = 552n) report that they had seriously considered leaving their institution. This is significantly lower than their Black peers who are heterosexual (n = 3,368, 38.3 percent, $\chi 2$ = 17.4p, p < .001n), as well as

Table 5.5 Seriously Considered Leaving, Multiple Identity Marker Comparisons

Intersectional Identity	N	Seriously Considered Leaving	Did Not Seriously Consider Leaving	Chi-square
White Women				
White x Woman	30,364	8,054 (26.5)	22,310 (73.5)	$\chi2$ (1) = 0.163
White x Man	15,333	4,040 (26.3)	11,293 (73.7)	$p = 0.686$
				$n = 45{,}697$
White x Woman	30,364	8,054 (26.5)	22,310 (73.5)	$\chi2$ (1) = 251.07
Minority x Woman	13,987	4,736 (33.9)	9,251 (66.1)	$p < .001$
				$n = 44{,}351$
White Heterosexual				
White x Heterosexual	38,983	9,835 (25.2)	29,148 (74.8)	$\chi2$ (1) = 240.36
White x Queerspectrum	6,026	2,091 (34.7)	3,935 (65.3)	$p < .001$
				$n = 45{,}009$
White x Heterosexual	38,983	9,835 (25.2)	29,148 (74.8)	$\chi2$ (1) = 261.51
Minority x Heterosexual	16,923	5,391 (31.9)	11,532 (68.1)	$p < .001$
				$n = 55{,}906$

(Continued)

Table 5.5 (Continued)

Intersectional Identity	N	Seriously Considered Leaving	Did Not Seriously Consider Leaving	Chi-square
Black Queerspectrum				
Black x Queerspectrum	552	263 (47.6)	289 (52.4)	$\chi2$ (1) = 17.42
Black x Heterosexual	3,368	1,289 (38.3)	2,079 (61.7)	$p < .001$
				$n = 3,920$
Black x Queerspectrum	552	263 (47.6)	289 (52.4)	$\chi2$ (1) = 36.88
White x Queerspectrum	6,026	2,091 (34.7)	3,935 (65.3)	$p < .001$
				$n = 6,578$
Minority Transpectrum				
Minority x Transpectrum	518	222 (42.9)	296 (57.1)	$\chi2$ (1) = 23.14
Minority x Cisgender	21,089	6,916 (32.8)	14,173 (67.2)	$p < .001$
				$n = 21,607$
Minority x Transpectrum	518	222 (42.9)	296 (57.1)	$\chi2$ (1) = 34.16
White x Transpectrum	829	309 (37.3)	520 (62.7)	$p < .05$
				$n = 6,578$

Note: N values may differ from previous tables. Respondents were not required to answer the question "Have you ever seriously considered leaving [institution]?"

significantly lower than their queerspectrum peers who are white (n = 6,026, 34.7 percent, $\chi 2 = 36.9p$, $p < .001$).

Racially Minoritized Transpectrum. Among minority transpectrum students (n = 518n), 42.9 percent report that they seriously considered leaving their institution. This is a significantly greater percentage than their minority peers who are Cisgender (n = 21,089), where nearly one-third (32.8 percent) reported that they had seriously considered leaving ($\chi 2 = 23.1p$, $p < .001n$). Additionally, minority transpectrum students report that they seriously considered leaving at significantly higher rates than their white transpectrum peers (n = 829, 37.3 percent, $\chi 2 = 4.2p$, $p < .05$).

Students who answered "yes" to "Have you ever seriously considered leaving [institution]?" were provided an opportunity to select *why* they may have considered leaving. Among students who reported that they had indeed seriously considered leaving their institution, the most reported reason was "lack of sense of belonging" (50.5 percent). Other top reasons were "lack of social life" (35.4 percent) and for "personal reasons" (28.5 percent) or "financial reasons" (27.8 percent). "Lack of a sense of belonging" was also the most reported reason among Black queerspectrum students (60.7 percent) and racially minoritized transpectrum students (62.4 percent); however, the second most reported reason for both populations was because the "campus climate was unwelcoming" (41.1 percent and 51.6 percent, respectively). Finally, significantly higher percentages of Black queerspectrum and racially minoritized transpectrum students reported they also seriously considered leaving owing to a "lack of a support group" (34.0% and 48.3 percent, respectively) and a lack of support services (26.8 percent and 31.9 percent, respectively).

Discussion

The findings from the study contribute to the professional literature on how higher education institutional climates shaped students' experiences differently based on one or more identity markers. Overall, our findings demonstrate that there are significant connections between undergraduate students' single and multiple, intersecting identity markers and reported sense of belonging, as well as between students' sense of belonging and intent to persist:

- Among single identity markers, women and white students have the highest sense of belonging, while transpectrum and Black students have the lowest sense of belonging.
- When evaluating intersectional identities, Black and multiracial transpectrum students have the lowest sense of belonging, followed by Black women.
- Black queerspectrum and transpectrum students of color seriously considering leaving their colleges or universities at significantly higher rates than their peers.

Although numerous statistical differences exist across the variables examined, we delve deeper into those associated with our research questions including gender, race, sexual identity, sense of belonging, and intent to leave as they relate to our three research questions.

Question 1: Sense of Belonging, Race, Gender, and Sexual Identity (as Single Identities)

First, findings highlighted varying levels of sense of belonging when groups were compared by single identity markers (race, gender identity, and sexual identity). Transpectrum students indicated the lowest sense of belonging and women students had the highest sense of belonging when compared to other groups. Since hostile campus climates for transpectrum students are associated with isolation and disengagement from others, our findings support the professional literature that higher education institutions are not creating enough spaces where transpectrum students can develop meaningful and authentic relationships that help buffer the negative effects of an unwelcoming campus climate (Gano, 2021).

Our findings also revealed that Black students had substantially lower sense of belonging while white students had the highest sense of belonging. This aligns with the research that underscores Black students' experiences with racism in the form of overt discrimination and ongoing microaggressions that have a negative impact on whether they fit in and connect to campus (Duran et al., 2020; Harper & Hurtado, 2007; Johnson, 2013). This finding further substantiates the concern that colleges and universities are "inherently privileging those from dominant groups" (Duran et al., 2020) while not creating or effectively managing resources and programs that increase same-race peer interactions such as Black cultural centers (Patton, 2006) and racial identity focused clubs and organizations (Harper & Quaye, 2007), and affirming and validating interactions and messages from faculty and staff (Newman et al., 2015).

A deeper exploration into within-group differences of these single identity markers revealed additional meaningful characteristics related to belonging that should be noted. Latine and AAPI students share their responses to a less welcoming campus climate; that is, they might conform or assimilate rather than challenge the majority culture on campus (Hurtado & Ponjuan, 2005; McGee, 2016; Yi & Todd, 2022) resulting in a sense of belonging that more closely resembles that of their white peers. In our study, the main differences in sense of belonging were found between white students and Black students and white students and Multiracial students; no significant differences emerged between AAPI and Latine students. Queerspectrum students in our study also indicated a lower sense of belonging than their heterosexual peers. Since belonging correlates to positive experiences on campus, queerspectrum students remain at risk for a lack of belonging due to their experiences with hostile campuses, physical and verbal abuse and microaggressions (Hughes & Hurtado, 2018; Tetreault et al., 2013).

Question 2: Sense of Belonging, Race, Gender, and Sexual Identity (as Intersectional Identities)

Second, a move from single identity markers to multiple identity markers revealed additional information related to sense of belonging. Black and multiracial transpectrum students had the lowest sense of belonging. Black women had the second lowest sense of belonging, with Black and multiracial men following with the third lowest sense of belonging. These findings bring to light the exponential impact of the intersection of race and gender in higher education. Black undergraduates who hold intersectional identities face a compounding effect of marginalization that results in lower sense of belonging (Strayhorn, 2019). Once again, in comparison, we found similar reported higher rates of sense of belonging between white, Latine, and AAPI undergraduates regardless of gender.

Findings also revealed the salient vulnerability associated with holding a transpectrum identity, regardless of sexual identity, in higher education and the urgency for colleges and universities to better meet the academic, social, and psychological needs of transpectrum undergraduates. Transpectrum undergraduates seem to be most disconnected from supportive relationships and programming often found in LGBTQ+ resource centers (Vaccaro & Newman, 2017) that would reduce the impact of a discriminatory campus climate. Queerspectrum undergraduates also remain vulnerable, regardless of race, due to similar risk factors faced by transpectrum undergraduates (Vaccaro & Newman, 2017).

Question 3: Sense of Belonging and Seriously Considered Leaving for Black Queerspectrum Students and Transpectrum Students of Color

Third, further analyses of select multiple identity marker groups revealed relationships between sense of belonging and intent to persist at higher education institutions. Research on sense of belonging highlights its relationship to persistence among Black undergraduate women (Booker, 2016; Walpole et al., 2014), Black undergraduate men (Kim & Hargrove, 2013; Palmer et al., 2014), Latine students (García & Garza, 2016; Heredia et al., 2018; Tovar, 2015), and queerspectrum and transpectrum individuals (Blumenfeld et al., 2016).

Nearly half of Black queerspectrum students in this study reported that they have seriously considered leaving their institutions. Transpectrum students of color seriously considered leaving at significantly higher rates than cisgender students of color and white transpectrum students. Top reasons why Black queerspectrum students and transpectrum students of color seriously considered leaving include a lack of a sense of belonging, climate not welcoming, and lack of social life. The rates of these reasons differed substantially when compared to all undergraduate students, suggesting the campus environment played a major role in their belonging and contemplation to leave. From these findings, we again see the exponential impact on undergraduate student well-being and progression when racialized undergraduate students also hold a minoritized gender or sexual identity. These findings fill intersectional identity gaps in the professional literature and call for urgent actions by colleges and universities to address the vulnerability and risk for Black queerspectrum students and transpectrum students of color.

Other findings to note include Women of color undergraduates (AAPI, Black, Latine, and multiracial) more often seriously considered leaving their institutions than white women undergraduates. The trend of compound marginalization extends to this finding in that being a woman and a person of color increases one's risk of leaving.

Campus Resources Discussion

Based on information from the prior literature review and this research study, it is imperative that colleges and universities reconceptualize their campus services toward more complex intersectional identities and more informal operational strategies. Whereas often colleges and universities respond to calls for inclusion with additional offices and services, the literature and this research strongly suggest that undergraduate students from minoritized groups seek opportunities to connect, characterized as authentic relationships, with other students, faculty, and staff. The hiring of faculty and staff who provide undergraduates with experiences of connectedness and social support is crucial to an increased sense of belonging. Beyond the creation of official organizational units that provide campus-based services, the hiring of *sense of belonging ambassadors* who authentically connect with students who hold single and intersectional minoritized identities would contribute in positive ways to the overall campus community. Historically, higher education student support units have focused nearly exclusively on single identity markers (e.g., race, gender, sexual identity). The literature and this study show the compounding effects of multiple minoritizing identity markers where sense of belonging and intent to persist are lower when compared with majority peers. Campus support resources must begin to reconceptualize their work around intersectional identities, particularly those that compound oppression and marginalization. This reconceptualization might begin with serious discussions about who benefits most (and least) when support units are focused on single identity markers. Reframing might begin with new unit names, programs, and services that draw in these diverse student subpopulations.

Students who cope with stress from multiple minoritized identities, in addition to the common stress experienced by undergraduate students, might not want to stay on campuses where they do not feel supported or seen. Based on the research literature and this study, these students are likely unable to find authentic, positive, and affirming interactions with similarly identifying peers and experience their campuses as hostile and unwelcoming. This study, and others in the literature, are unequivocal that colleges and universities continue to privilege already dominant groups while failing to create curricular, co-curricular, and extracurricular programs that account for marginalization and multiple identities. *End state strategies*, where universities create diversity units that support single marginalized identities, are necessary because of overall unwelcoming and hostile climates but are limited at best. Based on our findings, we recommend *core state strategies* whereby campus resources are directed utilizing more fluid and nuanced methods toward those who are most likely to lack a sense of belonging. Such core state strategies can flow from reconceptualized programs, curricula, and campus services that place cultural knowledge at the center of their work, are dynamic, and start with the basic and fundamental human need to belong.

Conclusion

This study draws from feminist standpoint and intersectional theories to advance the literature on sense of belonging, particularly as it relates to reconceptualizing campus resources for students marginalized by multiple identity markers. As a result of the evidence presented in this chapter, college and university leaders and educational scholars have additional knowledge about the impact of campus climate on undergraduate students' sense of belonging and their intent to persist (e.g., seriously considered leaving). Future research should continue to examine intersectional identities by different institutional types, regions, and majors, as well as utilize mixed-methods research to understand the relationships more fully between single and multiple marginalized identities, persistence and departure, and sense of belonging. Quantitative studies that are informed by feminist standpoint theory and intersectional methodologies offer more nuanced insights into the types of campus resources that best support contemporary marginalized identities of undergraduate students. It is intersectional research that helps create mosaics of experiences, ones where researchers and practitioners gain understanding of undergraduate student populations grounded in their multiple, different social locations.

References

Bejarano, C., & Valverde, M. (2012). From the fields to the university: Charting educational access and success for farmworker students using a community cultural wealth framework. *Journal of the Association of Mexican American Educators*, *6*(2), 22–29.

Blackmon, Z. R., O'Hara, R. M., & Viars, J. W. (2020). Microaggressions, sense of belonging, and sexual identity in the residential environment. *Journal of College and University Student Housing*, *46*(3), 46–59.

Blumenfeld, W. J., Weber, G. N., & Rankin, S. (2016). In our own voice: Campus climate as a mediating factor in the persistence of LGBT students, faculty, and staff in higher education. In E. A. Mikulec & P. C. Miller (Eds.), *Queering classrooms: Personal narratives and educational practices to support LGBTQ youth in schools* (pp. 187–212). IAP Information Age Publishing.

Booker, K. (2016). Connection and commitment: How sense of belonging and classroom community influence degree persistence for African American undergraduate women. *International Journal of Teaching & Learning in Higher Education*, *28*(2), 218–229.

Brooms, D. R. (2020). Helping us think about ourselves: Black males' sense of belonging through connections and relationships with faculty in college, *International Journal of Qualitative Studies in Education*, *33*(9), 921–938. https://doi.org/10.1080/09518398.2019.1687956

Budge, S. L., Domínguez, S., Jr., & Goldberg, A. E. (2020). Minority stress in nonbinary students in higher education: The role of campus climate and belongingness. *Psychology of Sexual Orientation and Gender Diversity*, *7*(2), 222–229. https://doi.org/10.1037/sgd0000360

Crenshaw, K. (1989). Demarginalizing the intersection of race and sex: A Black feminist critique of antidiscrimination doctrine, feminist theory and antiracist politics. *University of Chicago Legal Forum*, *1989*(1), 139–167.

Dortch, D., & Patel, C. (2017). Black undergraduate women and their sense of belonging in STEM at predominantly White institutions. *NASPA Journal About Women in Higher Education*, *10*(2), 202–215. https://doi.org/10.1080/19407882.2017.1331854

Duran, A. (2019). Queer and of color: A systematic literature review on queer students of color in higher education scholarship. *Journal of Diversity in Higher Education, 12*(4), 390–400. https://doi.org/10.1037/dhe0000084

Duran, A., Dahl, L. S., Stipeck, C., & Mayhew, M. J. (2020). A critical quantitative analysis of students' sense of belonging: Perspectives on race, generation status, and collegiate environments. *Journal of College Student Development, 61*(2), 133–153. https://doi.org/10.1353/csd.2020.0014.

Gano, B. (2021). *The experiences, thoughts, feelings, and emotions LGBTQ+ college students associate with sense of belonging* (Publication No. 28419611) [Doctoral dissertation, the University of North Carolina at Wilmington]. ProQuest Dissertations & Theses Global.

García, Hugo A., & Garza, T. (2016). Retaining Latino males in community colleges: A structural model explaining sense of belonging through socio-academic integration. *The Journal of Applied Research in the Community College, 23*(2), 41–58.

Good, C., Rattan, A., & Dweck, C. S. (2012). Why do women opt out? Sense of belonging and women's representation in mathematics. *Journal of Personality and Social Psychology, 102*(4), 700–717. https://doi.org/10.1037/a0026659

Gonyo, C. P. (2016). *The sense of belonging of Black gay men at predominantly White institutions of higher education* [Doctoral Dissertation: Michigan State University]. MSU Libraries Digital Repository. https://d.lib.msu.edu/etd/4401

Gopalan, M., & Brady, S. T. (2020). College students' sense of belonging: A national perspective. *Educational Researcher, 49*(2), 134–137. https://doi.org/10.3102/0013189X19897622

Harper, S. R., & Hurtado, S. (2007). Nine themes in campus racial climates and implications for institutional transformation. *New Directions for Student Services, 2007*, 7–24. https://doi.org/10.1002/ss.254

Harper, S. R., & Quaye, S. J. (2007). Student organizations as venues for black identity expression and development among African American male student leaders. *Journal of College Student Development, 48*(2), 127–144. https://doi.org/10.1353/csd.2007.0012.

Heredia, Jr., D., Piña-Watson, B., Castillo, L. G., Ojeda, L., & Cano, M. Á. (2018). Academic non-persistence among Latina/o college students: Examining cultural and social factors. *Journal of Diversity in Higher Education, 11*(2), 192–200.

Hughes, B. E., & Hurtado, S. (2018). Thinking about sexual orientation: College experiences that predict identity salience. *Journal of College*

Student Development, *59*(3), 309–326. https://doi.org/10.1353/csd.2018.0029.

Hurtado, S., Alvarez, C. L., Guillermo-Wann, C., Cuellar, M., & Arellano, L. (2012). A model for diverse learning environments. In J. Smart & M. Paulsen (Eds.), *Higher education: Handbook of* theory *and* research (Vol. 27). Dordrecht: Springer. https://doi.org/10.1007/978-94-007-2950-6_2

Hurtado, S., & Ponjuan, L. (2005). Latino educational outcomes and the campus climate. *Journal of Hispanic Higher Education*, *4*(3), 235–251. https://doi.org/10.1177/1538192705276548

Irwin, V., De La Rosa, J., Wang, K., Hein, S., Zhang, J., Burr, R., Roberts, A., Barmer, A., Bullock Mann, F., Dilig, R., & Parker, S. (2022). *Report on the condition of education 2022* (NCES 2022–144). U.S. Department of Education. Washington, DC: National Center for Education Statistics. Retrieved June 12, 2023 from https://nces.ed.gov/pubsearch/pubsinfo.asp?pubid=2022144.

Johnson, D. R. (2012). Campus racial climate perceptions and overall sense of belonging among racially diverse women in STEM majors. *Journal of College Student Development*, *53*(2), 336–346. https://doi.org/10.1353/csd.2012.0028

Johnson, D. R., Soldner, M., Leonard, J. B., Alvarez, P., Inkelas, K. K., Rowan-Kenyon, H., & Longerbeam, S. (2007). Examining sense of belonging among first-year undergraduates from different racial/ethnic groups. *Journal of College Student Development*, *48*(5), 525–542. https://doi.org/10.1353/csd.2007.0054

Johnson, I. R., Pietri, E. S., Fullilove, F., & Mowrer, S. (2019). Exploring identity-safety cues and allyship among Black women students in STEM environments. *Psychology of Women Quarterly*, *43*(2), 131–150. https://doi.org/10.1177/0361684319830926

Johnson, R. M. (2013). Black and male on campus: An autoethnographic account. *Journal of African American Males in Education*, *4*(2), 103–123.

Kim, E., & Hargrove, D. T. (2013). Deficient or resilient: A critical review of Black male academic success and persistence in higher education. *Journal of Negro Education*, *82*(3), 300–311. https://doi-org.ezproxy.hofstra.edu/10.7709/jnegroeducation.82.3.0300

Lather, P. (1992). Critical frames in educational research: Feminist and post-structural perspectives. *Theory Into Practice*, *31*(2), 87–99. https://doi.org/10.1080/00405849209543529

Lewis, J. A., Mendenhall, R., Ojiemwen, A., Thomas, M., Riopelle, C., Harwood, S. A., & Browne Huntt, M. (2021). Racial microaggressions and sense of belonging at a historically white University. *American Behavioral Scientist, 65*(8), 1049–1071. https://doi.org/10.1177/0002764219859613

Maramba, D. C. (2008). Immigrant families and the college experience perspectives of Filipina Americans. *Journal of College Student Development, 49*(4), 336–350. https://doi.org/10.1353/csd.0.0012

Maramba, D. C., & Museus, S. D. (2012). Examining the effects of campus climate, ethnic group cohesion, and cross-cultural interaction on Filipino American students' sense of belonging in college. *Journal of College Student Retention: Research, Theory and Practice, 14*(4), 495–522. https://doi.org/10.2190/CS.14.4.d

Master, A., & Meltzoff, A. (2020). Cultural stereotypes and sense of belonging contribute to gender gaps in STEM. *International Journal of Gender, Science and Technology*, 12(1), 152–198.

McGee, E. O. (2016). Devalued Black and Latino racial identities: A by-product of STEM college culture? *American Educational Research Journal, 53*(6), 1626–1662. https://doi.org/10.3102/0002831216676572

Mooney, C., & Becker, B. A. (2020). *Sense of belonging: The intersectionality of self-identified minority status and gender in undergraduate computer science students.* Proceedings of the UKICER '20 United Kingdom and Ireland Computing Education Research, 24–30. https://doi.org/10.1145/3416465.3416476

Museus, S. D., & Truong, K. A. (2009). Disaggregating qualitative data from Asian American college students in campus racial climate research and assessment. *New Directions for Institutional Research, 142*, 17–26. https://doi.org/10.1002/ir.293

Naples, N. A., & Gurr, B. (2013). Feminist empiricism and standpoint theory: Approaches to understanding the social world. In S. Nagy Hesse-Biber (Ed.), *Feminist research practice: A primer.* Sage Publications.

Newman, C. B., Wood, J. L., & Harris III, F. (2015). Black men's perceptions of sense of belonging with faculty members in community colleges. *Journal of Negro Education, 84*(4), 564–577. https://www.muse.jhu.edu/article/802819.

Nguyen, B. M., Nguyen, M. H., Chan, J. C., & Teranishi, R. T. (2016). *The racialized experiences of Asian American and pacific Islander students: An examination of campus racial climate at the University of California, Los Angeles.* iCount: A Data Quality Movement for Asian Americans and Pacific Islanders.

Nguyen, M. H., Chan, J., Nguyen, B. M. D., & Teranishi, R. T. (2018). Beyond compositional diversity: Examining the campus climate experiences of

Asian American and Pacific Islander students. *Journal of Diversity in Higher Education*, *11*(4), 484–501. https://doi.org/10.1037/dhe0000071

Nuñez, A. M. (2009). A critical paradox? Predictors of latino students' sense of belonging in college. *Journal of Diversity in Higher Education*, *2*(1), 46–61. https://doi.org/10.1037/a0014099

O'Keeffe, P. (2013). A sense of belonging: Improving student retention. *College Student Journal*, *47*(1), 605–613.

Palmer, R. T., Wood, J. L., Dancy, T. E., & Strayhorn, T. L. (2014). *Black male collegians: Increasing access, retention, and persistence in higher education: ASHE higher education report* (Vol. 40, No. 3), Wiley.

Parker, E. (2021). Campus climate perceptions and sense of belonging for LGBTQ students: A Canadian case study. *Journal of College Student Development*, *62*(2), 248–253. https://doi.org/10.1353/csd.2021.0019

Patton, L. D. (2006). Black culture centers: Still central to student learning. *About Campus*, *11*(2), 2–8. https://doi.org/10.1002/abc.160

Pinar, W. (2019). *What is curriculum theory?* (3rd ed.). Routledge. https://doi.org/10.4324/9781315625683

Rainey, K., Dancy, M., Mickelson, R., Stearns, E., & Moller, S. (2018). Race and gender differences in how sense of belonging influences decisions to major in STEM. *International Journal of STEM Education*, *5*(1), 10. https://doi.org/10.1186/s40594-018-0115-6

Rankin, S., Garvey, J. C., & Duran, A. (2019). A retrospective of LGBT issues on US college campuses: 1990–2020. *International Sociology*, *34*(4), 435–454. https://doi.org/10.1177/0268580919851429

Rankin, S., & Reason, R. (2008). Transformational tapestry model: A comprehensive approach to transforming campus climate. *Journal of Diversity in Higher Education*, *1*(4), 262–274. https://doi.org/10.1037/a0014018

Rodriguez, S. L., & Blaney, J. M. (2021). "We're the unicorns in STEM": Understanding how academic and social experiences influence sense of belonging for Latina undergraduate students. *Journal of Diversity in Higher Education*, *14*(3), 441–455. https://doi.org/10.1037/dhe0000176

Slaten, C. D., Elison, Z. M., Lee, J. Y., Yough, M., & Scalise, D. (2016). Belonging on campus: A qualitative inquiry of Asian international students. *The Counseling Psychologist*, *44*(3), 383–410. https://doi.org/10.1177/0011000016633506

Strayhorn, T. L. (2019). *College students' sense of belonging a key to educational success for all students* (2nd ed.). Routledge. https://doi.org/10.4324/9781315297293

Strayhorn, T. L., Lo, M.-T., Travers, C. S., & Tillman-Kelly, D. L. (2015). Assessing the relationship between well-being, sense of belonging, and confidence in the transition to college for black male collegians. *Spectrum: A Journal on Black Men*, *4*(1), 127–138. https://doi.org/10.2979/spectrum.4.1.07

Strayhorn, T. L. (2008). Sentido de pertenencia: A hierarchical analysis predicting sense of belonging among Latino college students. *Journal of Hispanic Higher Education, 7*(4), 301–320.

Tetreault, P. A., Fette, R., Meidlinger, P. C., & Hope, D. (2013). Perceptions of campus climate by sexual minorities. *Journal of Homosexuality, 60*(7), 947–964. https://doi.org/10.1080/00918369.2013.774874

Tovar, E. (2015). The role of faculty, counselors, and support programs on Latino/a community college students' success and intent to persist. *Community College Review*, *43*(1), 46–71.

Tsui, L. (2000). Effects of campus culture on students' critical thinking. *The Review of Higher Education*, *23*(4), 421–441. https://doi.org/10.1353/rhe.2000.0020.

Vaccaro, A., & Newman, B. M. (2016). Development of a sense of belonging for privileged and minoritized students: An emergent model. *Journal of College Student Development*, *57*(8), 925–942. https://doi.org/10.1353/csd.2016.0091.

Vaccaro, A., & Newman, B. M. (2017). A sense of belonging through the eyes of first-year LGBPQ students. *Journal of Student Affairs Research and Practices*, *54*(2), 137–149. https://doi.org/10.1080/19496591.2016.1211533

Valdez, Z., & Golash-Boza, T. (2020) Master status or intersectional identity? Undocumented students' sense of belonging on a college campus. *Identities*, 27(4), 481–499. https://doi.org/10.1080/1070289X.2018.1534452

Walpole, M., Chambers, C. R., & Goss, K. (2014). Race, class, gender and community college persistence among African American women. *NASPA Journal About Women in Higher Education*, *7*(2). https://doi.org/10.1515/njawhe-2014-0012

Wilson, L. C., & Liss, M. (2022). Safety and belonging as explanations for mental health disparities among sexual minority college students. *Psychology of Sexual Orientation and Gender Diversity*, *9*(1), 110–119. https://doi.org/10.1037/sgd0000421

Yi, J., & Todd, N. R. (2022). Race, campus climate, and social change behaviors for Asian American college students. *Journal of Diversity in Higher Education*, *15*(4), 453–465. https://doi.org/10.1037/dhe0000309

6

Centering Relationships

Belongingness in the Context of Religious, Spiritual, and Secular Identities, Perceptions, and Experiences

Matthew J. Mayhew, Musbah Shaheen, and Christa E. Winkler

Chapter Outline

Can religious, spiritual, and secular belongingness occur in the absence of spaces dedicated for safe worldview expression or when faculty and staff do not accommodate religious, spiritual, and secular needs with regard to celebrating holidays and other important in-kind observances? Driven by intersectionality frameworks responsibly stewarded by the work of Crenshaw (1991) and, more recently, Núñez (2014), we examine the collegiate conditions and educational practices that influence students' sense of religious, spiritual, and secular belongingness on college campuses.

What does it mean for college students to experience a sense of belonging on campus? Decades of empirical research on sense of belonging have demonstrated that belongingness is complex, influenced by one's social identities (Strayhorn, 2018), and driven by dynamics of power and privilege (Palmer & Strayhorn, 2008; Strayhorn, 2014a). Although researchers have focused on aspects of belongingness related to racial and ethnic identities (Klasik & Strayhorn, 2018; Strayhorn, 2010, 2020a), gender (Budge et al., 2020; Porter, 2022; Swisher, 2019), and sexuality (Budge et al., 2020; Garvey et al., 2018; Garvey & Kurotsuchi Inkelas, 2012), little research has focused on religious, secular, and spiritual (RSS) identities and experiences and their relationship to students' experiences of belongingness on campus.

Specifically, we use the extent to which students reported their campuses offering spaces for support and spiritual expression as a conceptual proxy and operational indicator of students' sense of belonging. Strayhorn (2018) defined postsecondary students' sense of belonging as "feeling cared about, accepted, respected, valued by, and important to the campus community or others on campus such as faculty, staff, or peers" (p. 4). Providing physical and psychological spaces for students to express their beliefs, engage with religious practices, and connect with RSS communities signals that the campus community values RSS identities and that students, especially those with minoritized religious identities, belong.

This chapter aims to examine the factors that influence students' perceptions of spaces for RSS support and expression on campus. We ask the following research question to guide this inquiry: How do collegiate conditions and educational practices influence students' sense of belonging as it relates to RSS identity expression? As part of answering this question, we will also explore how sense of belonging through RSS identity expression relates to interfaith behaviors and engagements and student interactions across RSS diversity and whether these relationships are influenced by RSS identities.

The analysis we conducted to address these issues has several advantages. First, the analysis uses weighted data to reflect the national composition of colleges and universities, and the weighted data allowed us to make nationally representative inferences. Second, the analysis adopted a multilevel approach that accounted for clustering across institutions and parsed out individual and institutional-level effects on belongingness. Finally, the analysis addressed how college graduates perceived their campuses over time, after their first year *and* during their last year in college. This longitudinal design provides information that educators need to improve how their institutions signal belongingness through providing and supporting safe spiritual expression on campuses for all students.

Background and Literature

In this chapter, we use intersectionality frameworks for framing our working understanding of sense of belonging as it relates to spiritual support and expression. To begin conversations relating to power, it is important to note that Christian hegemony is pervasive in US society and impacts every aspect of life (Edwards, 2017, 2021) and that the continued rise in Christian nationalist movements (Whitehead & Perry, 2020) signals the hold that Christianity has on the American people, including college students. With that in mind, the power that privileges Christianity simultaneously minoritizes other worldviews (e.g., Jews, Muslims). In other words, RSS worldviews do not hold equitable power, nor is their free expression welcomed and allowed to the same degree on college campuses (Ahmadi et al., 2019; Foste et al., 2021; Mayhew et al., 2022).

Therefore, the capacity of college campuses to provide spaces for support and spiritual expression signals to students from diverse RSS identities their belongingness to the campus community.

Space for support and spiritual expression, as we have operationalized in our previous research, has often been considered as a variable influencing interfaith learning and developmental outcomes, such as appreciative attitudes toward diverse others (Selznick et al., 2021; Shaheen et al., 2022), pluralism orientation (Rockenbach et al., 2015, 2016, 2017), and self-authored worldview commitment (Mayhew et al., 2016, 2020). Space for support and spiritual expression "is reflected in policies that provide religious accommodations, availability of groups or organizations for students to explore and express their worldviews, and the presence of campus educators to whom students can turn to support their worldview expression" (Rockenbach et al., 2017, p. 12). A campus community that signals student belongingness based on their RSS expressions is a safe place for students to express their worldviews, offers accommodations for students' needs with regard to celebrating religious holidays, and provides physical spaces to express worldviews.

Across all the research that emerged from the Interfaith Diversity Experiences and Attitudes Longitudinal Survey (IDEALS) project (Mayhew & Rockenbach, 2021), space for support and spiritual expression has emerged as a contributing factor to many outcomes related to interfaith learning and development. For example, when students who do not identify as Muslim perceive their campuses as a space for support and spiritual expression, they become more likely to appreciate Muslims by the end of their first year in college than when they first enrolled (Shaheen et al., 2022). Not only were spaces associated with appreciation, but the relationship between space and appreciation varied by RSS identity. For example, when Protestant students felt like they belonged on campus, they became more appreciative of Muslims than their peers. In another study, Mayhew et al. (2020) showed that "the power of free expression [of beliefs] appear[ed] to reduce students' inclinations to retreat and defend; where authenticity is endorsed and nurtured, students learn that they can commit to the beliefs and values that matter to them" (p. 20). Their findings underscore the positive connection between belongingness and identity (Strayhorn, 2012,

2014b) and reaffirm the need to examine belongingness as it relates to spiritual support and expression.

Few studies have focused on the connection between RSS identities and belonging. A notable exception is Strayhorn's (2018) work about the sense of belonging for gay men of color, of whom "a large majority reported [praying] as a way of making sense of their experiences and trying to establish a sense of belonging while in college" (p. 68). These studies make it clear that social identities (e.g., race, gender, sexual orientation, religion) converge and intersect in ways that influence the sense of belonging on campus. Therefore, our analysis of spaces for support and spiritual expression as components of belongingness remains a much-needed perspective for helping institutions serve diverse student populations.

Theoretical Framework

Intersectional thinking guided the study's framework. Based on the work of Crenshaw (1991) and Núñez (2014), we address the power embedded in hegemonic structures and their expressions by examining organizational levers as reasons for students' belongingness. In tandem, we fault the institutions for their inability to create conditions and enact equity-driven practices in cases where students voice a lack of belongingness. Indeed, equity-guided recommendations emerging from this effort are intended to equip educators with the information needed to disrupt white and Christian hegemonic structures and expression to make all students—including those minoritized racially and religiously—feel like they belong.

This study is grounded in the Interfaith Learning and Development (ILD) model presented by Mayhew and Rockenbach (2021) as a "responsible and timely theory-in-practice" for "thinking about religion and spirituality, students' approach to their own religious and spiritual selves and . . . the practices and developmental mechanisms needed to help students grow" (p. 2). To describe interfaith learning and development outcomes, the ILD postulates that growth in these areas is a function of the interfaith learning environment while accounting for student characteristics and pre-college experiences.

The ILD (Figure 6.1) describes the interfaith learning environment as nested spheres of influence. At the center are student engagements across RSS identities, both in the academic and social spaces. Engagements are couched within a disciplinary context (i.e., academic major), which is nested within a relational context. The outcome of this study, space for support and spiritual expression, is located within the relational context as an indicator of productive interpersonal interactions that facilitate a sense of belonging for students with diverse RSS identities and backgrounds. Along with it are other types of productive engagements (i.e., provocative encounters) as well as unproductive engagements (i.e., coercive, insensitive, negative), all of which contribute to shaping the relational context and influencing the collegiate environment.

These engagements and contexts are ultimately situated within an institutional context (i.e., organizational behaviors, campus conditions, climate, and culture) and, of course, a larger national context within which interfaith learning and development occurs. By accounting for these spheres of influence in the conceptualization of this study and analysis, the ILD provides a powerful theoretical perspective for examining how students experience mattering and belonging through the lens of RSS expression and support.

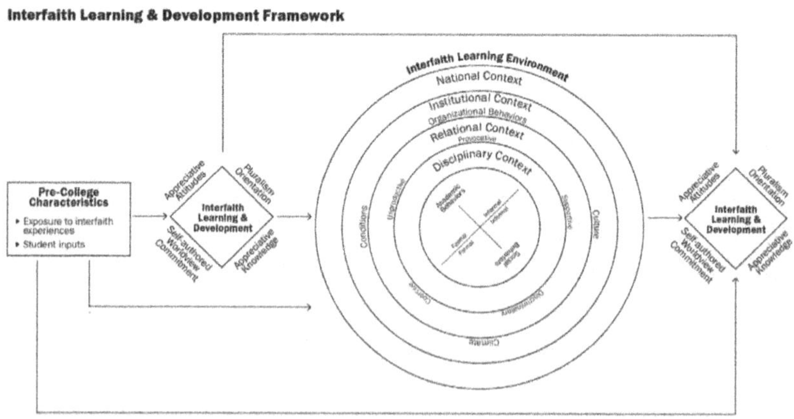

Figure 6.1 Interfaith Learning & Development Framework.

Methods

Data

Data were collected as part of the Interfaith Diversity Experiences and Attitudes Longitudinal Survey (IDEALS) project. The IDEALS survey—a theoretically derived and empirically validated measure of ILD—was administered longitudinally at 122 colleges and universities across the United States. The sample was stratified by institution type (i.e., Catholic, Evangelical, Mainline Protestant, private nonsectarian, and public), geographic region, selectivity, and affiliation (e.g., public, religiously affiliated, private nonsectarian). The survey included items capturing the institutional conditions and educational practices that influenced students' interfaith learning and development.

Administration of the survey was conducted over three separate time points to allow for the examination of students' longitudinal experiences and development during college. Responses were collected at the outset of students' college experience (summer or fall of 2015; $N = 20{,}436$), after students' first year in college (spring or fall of 2016; $N = 7{,}194$), and near the end of students' fourth year in college (spring of 2019; $N = 5{,}762$). Given our interest in understanding perceptions of on campus spaces that invited worldview expression, responses from students who participated in IDEALS at the second and third time points were used in these analyses, resulting in an analytic sample of 3,486 students at 122 institutions.

Measurement

The outcome variable in these analyses was students' perceptions of space for RSS support and expression on their campuses at the end of their fourth year in college. Variables measuring components of the ILD framework (Mayhew & Rockenbach, 2021)—including student inputs and behaviors and the interfaith learning environment—were measured and subsequently used as predictor variables.

Space for Support and Spiritual Expression

The outcome of interest, students' perceptions of space for support and spiritual expression, was measured via a theoretically derived and empirically validated scale comprised of four items: (1) This campus is a safe place for me to express my worldview; (2) Faculty and staff on my campus accommodate my needs with regard to celebrating holidays and other important observances connected to my religious or nonreligious worldview; (3) There is a place on this campus where I can express my personal worldview; and (4) My classes are safe places for me to express my worldview. Measure reliability was assessed for the analytic sample and deemed acceptable (T_2: $\alpha = 0.767$; T_3: $\alpha = 0.785$).

Student Inputs and Behaviors

Student-level variables were used to measure students' pre-college characteristics and pre-college exposure to interfaith experiences. The variables included to account for **students' pre-college characteristics** were gender identity, sexual orientation, race/ethnicity, worldview identification, education generation status, high school GPA, and political leaning. **Students' pre-college interfaith experiences** reflected the extent to which students engaged in interfaith activities before college. Thus, they were measured using a single composite score that captured the number of interfaith activities in which each student participated in the 12 months before beginning college. **Students' interfaith engagement behaviors** during college were disaggregated by formal (i.e., explicitly interfaith) or informal (i.e., not explicitly interfaith) and academic (i.e., curricular) or social (i.e., co-curricular). The number of formal academic, informal academic, formal social, and informal social activities in which students engaged was computed. Then, students were categorized as having participated in no activities (reference group), at least one activity, or two or more activities.

Interfaith Learning Environment

The interfaith learning environment was comprised of the national, institutional, relational, and disciplinary contexts in which students' interfaith experiences occurred on campus. The **institutional context** was measured with institution-level variables. Campus conditions included variables for institutional control (i.e., public versus private), selectivity (Barron's Profiles of American Colleges, NCES, 2015), and size of the undergraduate population. Organizational behaviors reflected the number of religious, spiritual, or interfaith programs, spaces, curricular opportunities, and diversity policies provided on campus, as reported by an institutional partner. Two campus climate indices (i.e., productive climate versus nonproductive climate for worldview diversity) and three campus culture indices (i.e., the ethos of an institution regarding its commitment to appreciative attitudes toward others' worldviews, pluralism orientation, and self-authored worldview commitment) were computed by averaging student-level perceptions to obtain an institution-level score. The **relational context** similarly included institution-level composite variables reflecting students' perceptions of insensitivity on campus, coercion on campus, unproductive interworldview engagement, and provocative experiences with worldview diversity. Finally, students' **disciplinary contexts** were included as a variable indicating the self-reported academic cluster in which their primary academic major was situated.

Analyses

Given the hierarchical nature of the data—with students clustered within 122 institutions—a multilevel modeling approach was used. The intraclass correlation coefficient (ICC), or the proportion of variance in the outcome accounted for by the nesting of students within institutions, was 0.0585. In other words, 5.85 percent of students' perceptions of space and support for RSS expression was accounted for by their institutional contexts. Although relatively small, the presence of an ICC above zero suggests that a multilevel approach is appropriate to account for non-independence of the data. Multilevel modeling allowed us to differentiate within-institution and between-institution variance in the model, thus more accurately estimating standard errors for a nested data structure (Raudenbush & Bryk, 2002). Additionally, normalized sampling weights were created using the Generalized Ranking Method (Deville et al., 1993) and applied to the analyses. Normalized weights were computed to adjust for response bias by gender, race, institutional type, Carnegie classification, geographic area, and urbanicity relative to the national landscape of higher education.

Application of those weights allowed us to make national claims based on findings from these analyses (See Table 6.1.).

Using multilevel modeling and weighted IDEALS survey data, we examined the student characteristics, campus engagement behaviors, and institutional conditions that contributed to increased space for spiritual expression and belonging between the end of students' first and fourth years of college. The outcome variable was the composite score measuring students' perceptions of space for support and spiritual expression on their campuses at the end of their fourth year in college. Variables measuring components of the ILD framework were included as predictor variables. Given our interest in understanding predictors of *increased* space for spiritual expression and belonging, the composite score measuring students' perceptions of space for support and spiritual expression on their campuses from the end of the first year of college was included as a control variable.

Following Mayhew and Simonoff (2015), we effect-coded multi-categorical variables in order to compare a value for one group (e.g., students who identify as holding a majority worldview) to the overall group mean of all students. As a result, rather than testing whether each group differs significantly from an arbitrary reference group, we tested whether all groups differed significantly from the overall sample mean. Effect coding was applied to students' gender, race, sexual orientation, worldview identification, political leaning, and academic field variables. Dummy coding was used for the institutional control variable (i.e., with private institutions relative to public institutions as the reference group) and student interfaith engagement behaviors (i.e., with at least one activity and two or more activities, related to no activities as the reference group). All continuous variables were standardized, with a mean of zero and a standard deviation of one, allowing results for those variables to be interpreted in effect size units.

Results from the multilevel model were interpreted based on *p*-values, regression coefficients, and model R^2. Parameter estimates with *p*-values less than .05 were considered statistically significant predictors of students' perceptions of space for support and spiritual expression at the end of college. Regression coefficients were used to understand the magnitude and direction of effects. Positive effects indicated variables associated with more positive perceptions relative to the end of the first year of college, while negative effects indicated variables associated with more negative

Table 6.1 *Multilevel Weighted Model for Space for Support and Spiritual Expression (N = 3486)*

	Est	SE	p
Control			
Space for support and spiritual expression at Time 2	0.279	0.020	* * *
Institutional campus climate			
Positive campus climate	0.003	0.042	
Negative campus climate	0.006	0.033	
Institutional campus culture			
Appreciative attitudes campus culture	0.038	0.065	
Pluralism campus culture	−0.078	0.044	
Self-authored worldview commitment campus culture	0.052	0.055	
Institutional campus conditions			
Undergraduate enrollment	0.032	0.021	
Selectivity	0.031	0.023	
Control (1 = Private; 0 = Public)	−0.012	0.073	
Institutional campus behaviors			
Total number of religious, spiritual, or interfaith programs provided on campus	0.027	0.024	
Total number of religious, spiritual, or interfaith spaces provided on campus	−0.015	0.020	
Total number of religious, spiritual, or interfaith curricular opportunities provided on campus	−0.051	0.021	*
Total number of religious, spiritual, or interfaith diversity policies provided on campus	−0.002	0.025	
Student identity characteristics and pre-college behaviors			
Pre-college interfaith activities	−0.044	0.024	
Gender			
Woman	−0.012	0.072	
Man	−0.071	0.068	
Another gender identity	0.082	0.132	
Sexual Orientation			
Bisexual	−0.191	0.092	*
Gay	0.000	0.143	
Heterosexual	0.017	0.051	
Lesbian	−0.013	0.084	
Queer	0.261	0.130	*
Another sexual orientation	−0.073	0.086	

(Continued)

Table 6.1 (Continued)

	Est	SE	p
Generation status (1 = First-generation; 0 = Continuing generation)	−0.006	0.064	
High school GPA	−0.018	0.023	
Race/ethnicity			
African American/Black	−0.215	0.070	**
Asian/Pacific Islander	0.054	0.054	
Latino	0.063	0.070	
White	0.061	0.045	
Other race	0.038	0.076	
Worldview identification			
Worldview majority	0.068	0.043	
Worldview minority	0.047	0.052	
Nonreligious worldview	0.055	0.063	
Another worldview	−0.171	0.110	
Political leaning			
Very conservative	0.167	0.112	
Conservative	−0.040	0.053	
Moderate	−0.034	0.045	
Liberal	−0.045	0.049	
Very liberal	−0.048	0.080	
Disciplinary context			
Arts, Humanities, or Religion	0.154	0.073	*
Social Science or Education	−0.046	0.071	
Health	−0.049	0.065	
Science, Math, or Engineering	−0.043	0.040	
Business	−0.089	0.081	
Undecided or another major	0.072	0.054	
Relational context			
Insensitivity on campus	−0.078	0.037	*
Coercion on campus	−0.289	0.038	***
Negative interworldview engagement	−0.169	0.032	***
Provocative encounters with worldview diversity	0.227	0.027	***
Student interfaith behaviors			
Formal academic engagement			
At least one activity (no activities as reference)	−0.039	0.091	
Two or more activities (no activities as reference)	−0.155	0.080	
Informal academic engagement			
At least one activity (no activities as reference)	0.085	0.047	
Two or more activities (no activities as reference)	0.165	0.050	***

(*Continued*)

Table 6.1 (Continued)

	Est	SE	p
Formal social engagement			
At least one activity (no activities as reference)	0.135	0.080	
Two or more activities (no activities as reference)	0.172	0.067	**
Informal social engagement			
At least one activity (no activities as reference)	−0.074	0.121	
Two or more activities (no activities as reference)	0.185	0.095	

$R^2 = 0.409$
* *p* < .05, ** *p* < .01, *** *p* < .001

perceptions relative to the end of the first year of college. The extent to which the model predicted students' perceptions of space for support and spiritual expression was evaluated based on R^2—a measure of the percentage variance in the criterion explained by the combination of all variables in the model.

Results

Altogether the variables included in the multilevel model explained 41 percent of the variance in the outcome of interest ($R^2 = .409$). In other words, the components of the ILD framework explained nearly half of the variation in students' perceptions of space for spiritual expression and belonging on campus near the conclusion of their fourth year in college. This model controlled for students' perceptions of space and support for spiritual expression near the end of their second year of college. Thus, results reflect changes in students' perceptions of space for spiritual expression and belonging between their second and fourth years of college.

With regard to student inputs, sexual orientation, and racial identity significantly predicted changes in the outcome. Specifically, students who identified as bisexual reported significantly less space for support and spiritual expression ($B = -0.191$, $p = .037$), while those who identified as queer reported significantly more space for support and spiritual expression ($B = 0.261$, $p = .045$) on campus.

Institutions also struggled to provide space and support for the spiritual expression of African American or Black students, *ceteris paribus*. Across RRS narratives, students who identified as African American or Black reported less space for support and spiritual expression on campus ($B = -0.215$, $p = .002$).

With regard to students' interfaith engagement behaviors on campus, both informal academic engagement and formal social engagement played a role. Students who participated in two or more informal academic engagement activities (e.g., dining, studying, or socializing with someone with a different RSS identity) reported increased space for support and spiritual expression ($B = 0.165$, $p = .001$). Similarly, students who participated in two or more formal social engagement activities reported increased space for support and spiritual expression ($B = 0.172$, $p = .010$).

With regard to the interfaith learning environment, the institutional context, relational context, and disciplinary context all significantly predicted changes in students' perceptions of space for spiritual expression and belonging on campus. Among the institutional context variables, only the number of curricular opportunities played a role in students' perceptions. More specifically, students attending campuses with more religious, spiritual, or interfaith curricular opportunities on campus reported somewhat decreased perceptions of campus as a space that invites and supports RSS expression ($B = -0.051$, $p = .015$). Finally, one cluster within the disciplinary context emerged as a significant predictor of space for spiritual expression and belonging. Students with primary academic majors in arts, humanities, or religion reported increased space for support and spiritual expression ($B = 0.154$, $p = .036$) on campus relative to their peers in other academic disciplines.

The relational context of the interfaith learning environment emerged as particularly salient, as all aspects of the relational context significantly predicted students' perceptions with regard to the outcome. Students who reported experiencing more insensitivity ($B = -0.078$, $p = .034$), coercion ($B = -0.289$, $p < .001$), and negative interworldview engagement ($B = -0.169$, $p < .001$) on campus also reported less space for support and spiritual expression. Conversely, students who experienced more provocative encounters with worldview diversity reported increased space for support and spiritual expression ($B = 0.227$, $p < .001$) on campus.

Discussion

Relationships clearly matter in the context of a sense of belonging linked to spiritual support and expression. Students who experienced interactions that were insensitive, coercive, or negative were less likely to report belonging on campus. In tandem, institutional campus climate, culture, and conditions did not predict sense of belonging in this study, a surprising result based on the documented work of others (e.g., Bowman et al., 2017; Mayhew et al., 2020; Rockenbach et al., 2017; Shaheen et al., 2022). Conversely, students who had encounters that evoked productive—and supported—dissonance became more likely to perceive their campus as a place where they belonged. As noted by Strayhorn (2018), "interactions with others that are affectively positive or pleasant are necessary . . . for experiencing belongingness" (p. 36). Taken together, these findings perhaps indicate that belonging is personal, perceived, and expressed through day-to-day interactions with peers, faculty, and staff. That said, the onus for belongingness should not fall on the students alone: institutions must examine their practice regarding the spaces they create to help students center relationships, especially as it relates to RSS diversity.

One place for creating space is through formal co-curricular opportunities for interfaith engagement. We found it intriguing that these formal co-curricular spaces (e.g., attending an interfaith vigil) were associated with increases in sense of belonging, but informal ones (e.g., dining with someone from a different religion) were not. In previous research, we have often seen exchanges occurring between peers in informal social contexts as critical for learning and developmental gains in outcomes related to religion, spirituality, and secularity (e.g., Mayhew et al., 2022; Selznick et al., 2021; Shaheen et al., 2022). Perhaps RSS belongingness is connected to and sustained in formalized co-curricular practice, as our findings also show that participating in at least two of these formal co-curricular activities is necessary for students to feel like they belong.

Similarly, two or more academic engagements also were associated with a sense of belonging. However, here informal engagements (e.g., brainstorming a solution to a societal issue by working with students from other religious or nonreligious perspectives, using a case study as a way to examine religious and nonreligious diversity in the world, discussing religious or spiritual topics with faculty) seemed more connected to it than formal ones (e.g., enrolling in a religion course).

Surprisingly, the total number of religious, spiritual, or interfaith curricular opportunities provided on campus was negatively related to students' RSS sense of belonging. This finding alongside the lack of significant effect of participating in formal interfaith academic engagements warrants two noteworthy considerations. First, curricular spaces may be doing more harm than good in providing a space for RSS support and healthy expression. Academic conversations that infuse RSS reflections are important. However, they must be done in ways that invite safe expression: As noted in previous research, educators "must establish empirical pathways for enabling students to exchange freely, equipped with the agency needed to have the provocative and seemingly uncomfortable encounters necessary for learning to occur" (Shaheen et at., 2022, p. 84). Otherwise, academic spaces fall short of reaching their potential positive impact on students' sense of belonging, especially in RSS contexts. Second, and relatedly, academic engagements associated with belongingness may need to center relationships *with* faculty as opposed to mere exposure *to* faculty through established curricular spaces. In other words, belongingness may be more related to the quality and depth of faculty interactions—something for future researchers to consider—than mere classroom exposure to the topic.

The associations between belongingness and engagement—either social or academic— were consistent for many students, regardless of student identities. Specifically, religious, spiritual, and secular identification, gender, generation status, political leaning, and high school grade point average were not associated with belonging on campus. Only three identification patterns emerged from this study as related empirically to RSS belongingness: sexual orientation, race, and college major.

The effect of sexual orientation was intriguing. Previous research has shown that queer- and trans-spectrum students tend to perceive their campuses as unwelcoming and are less likely to indicate feeling like they belonged (e.g., Garvey & Rankin, 2015; Rankin et al., 2019). This trend was true for bisexual students, whereas students who chose the label queer were more likely to perceive their belonging on campus. The lack of research in this area of belonging leaves us unable to describe more thoroughly the effects of sexual orientation on RSS belonging.

Regardless of worldview, political orientation, gender, sexual orientation, generation status, major, or GPA, African American/Black students were less likely to identify their campuses as spaces for RSS support and healthy expression than anyone else in the sample. This finding echoes previous research demonstrating how institutions continue to fail African American/Black students who perceive and experience them as hostile spaces where they do not belong (e.g., Strayhorn, 2017, 2020b; Strayhorn et al., 2015). Part of unpacking these experiences of disbelonging and marginalization involves an evolved notion of power, a construct stewarded responsibly by intersectional scholars like Crenshaw (1991) and Núñez (2014): Núñez (2014) notes the importance of "lay[ing] bare the dynamics of the organizational, representational, intersubjective, and experiential arenas of practice that influence students' educational opportunities according to various social identities, and . . . locat[ing] these arenas of practice within specific times and places" (Núñez, 2014, p. 90). The same power imbalances perpetuating racism might sustain Christian hegemony in and across higher education institutions within the American context—differentially affecting Black students, regardless of their RSS affiliations. How power associated with supremacy expressions is disrupted responsibly must continue to be underscored as an institutional priority, if we care about Black students and their sense of belonging, racially and religiously.

Finally, students who majored in arts, humanities, or religion were more likely to feel like they belonged on campus. Previous research regarding sense of belonging for college students has often focused on belonging in fields of study, such as STEM fields (e.g., Strayhorn et al., 2015) and business (e.g., Strayhorn, 2020a), that have excluded students with marginalized identities. Little research has explored belongingness, especially as it relates to RSS contexts, in other fields like arts, humanities, or religion. In the context of RSS belonging, our research shows that students who major in these areas seem to have more space to express their RSS worldviews safely, compared to other students in the study.

Implications

This study highlights how educators could foster a campus environment that signals belongingness across diverse RSS narratives. Attending religious services for a religious tradition that is not their own, participating in interfaith activity in conjunction with a service activity, living in an interfaith living-learning community, participating in a campus interfaith group, attending a formal debate on campus between people with different worldviews, among many other social programming activities (see Mayhew et al., 2020), are all positive contributors to belonging. Of course, attending two or more of these would be ideal, according to this study's findings.

On the academic side, many possible engagements can be arranged to promote belongingness. Examples include discussing religious or spiritual topics with faculty in classroom spaces, reflecting on why interfaith cooperation is relevant to their field of study, and developing a deeper skill set to interact with people of diverse religious and nonreligious perspectives. Importantly, participating in these engagements cannot be a one-and-done symbolic gesture but should be part of a sustained effort to keep students engaged in religious, secularity, and spirituality conversations. Perhaps experiences in arts, humanities, and religion disciplines could provide insights on how to engage productively with RSS conversations, given the positive association of these majors with belonging. Continued assessment of this outcome within these academic spaces could provide insights for other disciplines and demonstrate the value these disciplines offer for students' learning, development, and belonging.

The findings also have major implications for theory. Current theories regarding sense of belonging in the collegiate population often neglect—or even completely dismiss—RSS belongingness as a part of critical conversations on campus. Our findings suggest that this aspect of belonging could play a significant role in shaping students' experiences, especially Black students and students who hold other marginalized identities. Of course, future research should invite RSS elements into belongingness efforts as empirical work continues to document their powerful effect on student learning and development.

Conclusion

As an outgrowth of Strayhorn's (2018) powerful work on belongingness, this study locates its importance by examining belongingness in the context of religious, spiritual, and secular identities, perceptions, and experiences. Admittedly imperfect, our operation of belongingness in this context invoked space as its salient feature—space dedicated for students' safe religious, spiritual, and secular expression: The more students felt safe to express their ideas about religion on campus, the more they would feel a sense of belongingness on that campus.

As an extension of critical religious epistemology (Edwards, 2018; Small, 2020) and intersectionality frameworks that center power imbalance as potential means for oppression (See Museus & Griffin, 2011; Núñez, 2014), we recognize belongingness may be experienced differently based on being minoritized religiously in an American context where Christian nationalism is embedded, if not embraced. Although students' religious, spiritual, and secular identification patterns were not related directly to belongingness in this study, we would be remiss for not underscoring that certain narrative patterns—specifically related to sexual orientation and race—were, suggesting that minoritized status continues to share a curious and riddled relationship with belongingness.

Speaking of relationships, this study's main contribution involves its role in promoting belongingness within an RSS context. Relating with faculty in personal and professional ways in or out of the classroom and with others in formal co-curricular contexts were related to the development of RSS belongingness over time. Put simply, centering relationships matters in helping students belong with regard to religion, secularity, and spirituality.

References

Ahmadi, S., Sanchez, M., & Cole, D. (2019). Protecting Muslim students' speech and expression and resisting islamophobia. In D. L. Morgan & C. H. F. Davis (Eds.), *Student activism, politics, and campus climate in higher education* (1st ed., pp. 97–111). Routledge. https://doi.org/10.4324/9780429449178-6

Bowman, N. A., Rockenbach, A. N., Mayhew, M. J., Riggers-Piehl, T. A., & Hudson, T. D. (2017). College students' appreciative attitudes toward Atheists. *Research in High*, *1*, 98–118.

Budge, S. L., Domínguez Jr., S., & Goldberg, A. E. (2020). Minority stress in nonbinary students in higher education: The role of campus climate and belongingness. *Psychology of Sexual Orientation and Gender Diversity, 7*(2), 222–229. https://doi.org/10.1037/sgd0000360

Crenshaw, K. (1991). Mapping the margins: Intersectionality, identity politics, and violence against women of color. *Stanford Law Review, 43*(6), 1241. https://doi.org/10.2307/1229039

Deville, J., Särndal, C. E., & Sautory, O. (1993). Generalized ranking procedures in survey sampling. *Journal of the American Statistical Association, 88*(423), 1013–1020. https://doi.org/10.1080/01621459.1993.10476369

Edwards, S. (2017). Intergroup dialogue & religious identity: Attempting to raise awareness of Christian privilege & religious oppression. *Multicultural Education, 24*(2), 18–24.

Edwards, S. (2018). Critical reflections on the interfaith movement: A social justice perspective. *Journal of Diversity in Higher Education, 11*(2), 164–181. https://doi.org/10.1037/dhe0000053

Edwards, S. (2021). Religious "nones" and onto-epistemic socialization: Problematizing participant self-identification in research on religious identity. *Journal of College and Character, 22*(4), 291–306. https://doi.org/10.1080/2194587X.2021.1977150

Foste, Z., Staples, B. A., Durako Fisher, L. E., Shaheen, M., Mayhew, M. J., & Rockenbach, A. N. (2021). "Careful with your 'We'": Worldview minority faculty at sectarian institutions. *Journal of Diversity in Higher Education.* https://doi.org/10.1037/dhe0000320

Garvey, J. C., & Kurotsuchi Inkelas, K. (2012). Exploring relationships between sexual orientation and satisfaction with faculty and staff interactions. *Journal of Homosexuality, 59*(8), 1167–1190. Women's Studies International.

Garvey, J. C., & Rankin, S. (2015). The influence of campus experiences on the level of outness among trans-spectrum and queer-spectrum students. *Journal of Homosexuality, 62*(3), 374–393. https://doi.org/10.1080/00918369.2014.977113

Garvey, J. C., Squire, D. D., Stachler, B., & Rankin, S. (2018). The impact of campus climate on queer-spectrum student academic success. *Journal of LGBT Youth, 15*(2), 89–105. http://dx.doi.org/10.1080/19361653.2018.1429978

Klasik, D., & Strayhorn, T. L. (2018). The complexity of college readiness: Differences by race and college selectivity. *Educational Researcher, 47*(6), 334–351.

Mayhew, M. J., Hoggan, C., Rockenbach, A. N., & Lo, M. A. (2016). The association between worldview climate dimensions and college students' perceptions of transformational learning. *The Journal of Higher Education*, *87*(5), 674–700.

Mayhew, M. J., & Rockenbach, A. N. (2021). Interfaith learning and development. *Journal of College and Character*, *22*(1), 1–12. https://doi.org/10.1080/2194587X.2020.1860778

Mayhew, M. J., Rockenbach, A. N., & Dahl, L. S. (2020). Owning faith: First-year college-going and the development of students' self-authored worldview commitments. *The Journal of Higher Education*, 1–26. https://doi.org/10.1080/00221546.2020.1732175

Mayhew, M. J., Shaheen, M., & Staples, B. A. (2022). Redefining interfaith engagement: A case study of one evangelical institution. *Christian Higher Education*, 1–25. https://doi.org/10.1080/15363759.2022.2142989

Mayhew, M. J., & Simonoff, J. S. (2015). Non-white, no more: Effect coding as an alternative to dummy coding with implications for higher education researchers. *Journal of College Student Development*, *56*(2), 170–175. https://doi.org/10.1353/csd.2015.0019

Museus, S. D., & Griffin, K. A. (2011). Mapping the margins in higher education: On the promise of intersectionality frameworks in research and discourse. *New Directions for Institutional Research*, *2011*(151), 5–13. https://doi.org/10.1002/ir.395

National Center for Education Statistics (2015). *Barron's admissions competitiveness* index.

Núñez, A.-M. (2014). Employing multilevel intersectionality in educational research: Latino identities, contexts, and college access. *Educational Researcher*, *43*(2), 85–92. https://doi.org/10.3102/0013189X14522320

Palmer, R. T., & Strayhorn, T. L. (2008). Mastering one's own fate: Non-cognitive factors associated with the success of African American males at an HBCU. *NASAP Journal*, *11*(1), 126–143.

Porter, C. J. (2022). (Re)imagining belonging: Black women want more than survival in predominantly white institutions. *Journal of College Student Development*, *63*(1), 106–110. https://doi.org/10.1353/csd.2022.0002

Rankin, S., Garvey, J. C., & Duran, A. (2019). A retrospective of LGBT issues on US college campuses: 1990–2020. *International Sociology*, *34*(4), 435–454. https://doi.org/10.1177/0268580919851429

Raudenbush, S. W., & Bryk, A. S. (2002). *Hierarchical linear models: Applications and data analysis methods* (2nd ed.). SAGE.

Rockenbach, A. N., Mayhew, M. J., Correia-Harker, B. P., Morin, S., & Associates. (2017). *Navigating pluralism: How students approach religious difference and interfaith engagement in their first year of college*. Interfaith Youth Core.

Rockenbach, A. N., Mayhew, M. J., Davidson, J., Ofstein, J., & Bush, R. C. (2015). Complicating universal definitions: How students of diverse worldviews make meaning of spirituality. *Journal of Student Affairs Research and Practice, 52*(1), 1–10. https://doi.org/10.1080/19496591.2015.996058

Rockenbach, A. N., Riggers-Piehl, T. A., Garvey, J. C., Lo, M. A., & Mayhew, M. J. (2016). The influence of campus climate and interfaith engagement on self-authored worldview commitment and pluralism orientation across sexual and gender identities. *Research in Higher Education, 57*(4), 497–517. https://doi.org/10.1007/s11162-015-9395-6

Selznick, B. S., Mayhew, M. J., Dahl, L. S., & Rockenbach, A. N. (2021). Developing appreciative attitudes toward Jews: A multi-campus investigation. *The Journal of Higher Education*, 1–29. https://doi.org/10.1080/00221546.2021.1990632

Shaheen, M., Dahl, L. S., Mayhew, M. J., & Rockenbach, A. N. (2022). Inspiring Muslim appreciation in the first-year of college: What makes a difference? *Research in Higher Education*. https://doi.org/10.1007/s11162-022-09701-y, https://doi.org/10.1353/csd.2022.0007

Small, J. L. (2020). *Critical religious pluralism in higher education: A social justice framework to support religious diversity*. Routledge.

Strayhorn, T. L. (2010). When race and gender collide: Social and cultural capital's influence on the academic achievement of African American and Latino males. *The Review of Higher Education, 33*(3), 307–332.

Strayhorn, T. L. (2012). Exploring the impact of Facebook and Myspace use on first-year students' sense of belonging and persistence decisions. *Journal of College Student Development, 53*(6), 783–796.

Strayhorn, T. L. (2014a). What role does grit play in the academic success of black male collegians at predominantly white institutions? *Journal of African American Studies, 18*, 1–10.

Strayhorn, T. L. (2014b). Making a way to success: Self-authorship and academic achievement of first-year African American students at historically Black colleges. *Journal of College Student Development, 55*(2), 151–167.

Strayhorn, T. L. (2017). Factors that influence the persistence and success of Black men in urban public universities. *Urban Education, 52*(9), 1106–1128.

Strayhorn, T. L. (2018). *College students' sense of belonging: A key to educational success for all students*. Taylor & Francis Group. http://ebookcentral.proquest.com/lib/ohiostate-ebooks/detail.action?docID=5582832

Strayhorn, T. L. (2020a). Exploring the role of race in black males' sense of belonging in medical school: A qualitative pilot study. *Medical Science Educator, 30*(4), 1383–1387.

Strayhorn, T. L. (2020b). Measuring the relation between sense of belonging, campus leadership, and academic achievement for African American students at historically Black colleges and universities (HBCUs): A "gender equity" analysis. *Journal of Minority Achievement, Creativity, and Leadership, 1*(1), 94–118.

Strayhorn, T. L., Lo, M.-T., Travers, C. S., & Tillman-Kelly, D. L. (2015). Assessing the relationship between well-being, sense of belonging, and confidence in the transition to college for Black male collegians. *Spectrum: A Journal on Black Men, 4*(1), 127–138.

Swisher, S. B. (2019). *Gendered islamophobia and sense of belonging: Experiences of visibly Muslim women in higher education* (Ph.D.), Fordham University. http://search.proquest.com/docview/2160912714/abstract/47FFAD34E659403APQ/1

Whitehead, A. L., & Perry, S. L. (2020). *Taking America back for God: Christian nationalism in the United States.* Oxford University Press.

7

The Conditional Effects of Participating in a Student Organization on College Students' Sense of Belonging

Krista M. Soria, Erin Standley, and Justin Braun

Chapter Outline

Introduction

College students' sense of belonging—defined in this chapter as students' feelings of acceptance, value, and belonging at their colleges and universities—is a critical psychosocial dimension associated with students' retention, persistence, academic achievement, mental health, and development (Davis et al., 2019; Gopalan & Brady, 2020; Hoffman et al., 2002; Soria & Mitchell, 2015; Stephens et al., 2014; Strayhorn, 2019). Yet, because higher education institutions were designed by—and for—those from privileged backgrounds as a means of reproducing and validating existing social inequalities (Soria, 2015), institutional barriers, unwelcoming campus climates, and lack of sociocultural support leaves students from marginalized, minoritized, and systemically excluded backgrounds with a lower sense of belonging than their peers (Rodriguez & Blaney, 2021; Soria, 2015, 2018; Soria & Bultmann, 2014; Strayhorn, 2019).

Although sense of belonging is important for all students in higher education (Strayhorn, 2019), over the last several decades, researchers have documented that students from marginalized, minoritized, and systemically excluded backgrounds have significantly lower levels of sense of belonging compared to their more privileged or majority peers. For instance, students with racially and ethnically minorized identities, including Black, Hispanic, Latinx, Asian, Native American or Alaska Native, multiracial, and Native Hawaiian or Pacific Islander students are likely to experience a lower sense of belonging compared to white students at predominantly white institutions (Duran et al., 2020; Johnson et al., 2007; Lewis et al., 2021; Museus & Maramba, 2011; Museus et al., 2017; Soria & Alkire, 2015; Strayhorn, 2008a, 2008b, 2019; Tachine et al., 2017).

Additionally, working-class students and students from lower socioeconomic backgrounds tend to have a lower sense of belonging than middle- or upper-class students (Bettencourt, 2021; Soria & Bultmann, 2014; Soria et al., 2013–2014; Taylor et al., 2022). Bisexual, gay, lesbian, pansexual, and queer students also have a lower sense of belonging compared to heterosexual or straight students (Blakmon et al., 2020; BrckaLorenz et al., 2021; Dugan et al., 2012; Duran et al., 2020; Vaccaro & Newman, 2017). Transgender, genderqueer, and non-binary students tend to have a lower sense of belonging compared to cisgender students (Dugan et al., 2012; Duran et al., 2020). Further, first-generation college students—those whose parents have not earned a bachelor's degree or higher—are also likely to experience a lower sense of belonging compared to continuing-generation students (Duran et al., 2020; Soria & Stebleton, 2012; Stebleton et al., 2014). Finally, researchers have also demonstrated that students with disabilities tend to have a lower sense of belonging compared to students without disabilities (Soria, 2021).

Experiences with racism, classism, homophobia, transphobia, sexism, ableism, discrimination, and unwelcoming campus climates can lead to increased social isolation and alienation for some students, diminishing their feelings of belonging (Parker, 2021; Soria, 2018; Stebleton et al., 2014). Students who are systemically underrepresented on campuses may struggle to find others from similar backgrounds and life experiences, encounter an absence of relevant learning opportunities or representation in curriculum, and feel invalidated, all of which further diminishes their sense of belonging (Museus & Chang, 2021; Soria & Stebleton, 2013). Students from marginalized, minoritized, and systemically excluded backgrounds inherit different forms of sociocultural capital than is typically valued and rewarded in higher education, thus requiring them to tread carefully as they navigate the hidden curriculum of higher education and hide or alter aspects of their identity to pass or assimilate in the dominant higher education culture, often at the expense of their sense of belonging (Hurst, 2012; Soria, 2015; Strayhorn, 2019; Villalpando & Solórzano, 2005; Yosso, 2005).

While students' participation in campus clubs, groups, or organizations can elevate students' sense of belonging (Strayhorn, 2019; Vaccaro & Newman, 2016), at present, most quantitative research published about the potential effects of students' participation in student clubs, groups, or organizations is limited because students' self-selection biases have not been included in analytical models. Those self-selection biases can lead to systematic biases in the outcomes of students' participation (Soria et al., 2019a). In this chapter, we explored whether students' participation in at least one student organization can serve as a catalyst to disrupt systemic inequities in students' sense of belonging. Specifically, we examined whether students who participate in at least one student organization have a different sense of belonging compared to matched pairs of students who did not participate in a student organization. We further examined whether any differences are conditional by students' race/ethnicity, social class, sexual orientation, gender, first-generation status, and disability. To address the limitations of prior research, we used propensity score matching techniques to create matched pairs of students who did and did not participate in a student organization to better assess the potential benefits of students' participation in a student organization on their sense of belonging.

Our work is supported by Vaccaro and Newman's (2016) model of belonging for privileged and minoritized students, which suggests that students' involvement on campus can increase students' sense of belonging when students develop meaningful connections by being their authentic selves in student groups or organizations. The methodology is also supported by Astin's (1993) input-environment-output theory. Astin suggested that students' pre-college experiences and demographics (inputs) and experiences in higher education (environment) influences the outcomes students derive from programs on campus. Our statistical approach reflected Astin's model: we considered students' "input" variables (e.g., demographics) and other "environmental" collegiate experiences (e.g., students' residence, institutional size) when estimating the effects of students' participation in a student organization on their sense of belonging. We used input and environmental variables as covariates when constructing matched pairs of students who did and did not participate in a student organization at least once in their college experience.

The Study

Research Design

We utilized data from the Multi-Institutional Study of Leadership (MSL) survey, which was administered to undergraduate students at sixty-nine US four-year colleges and universities from January to May of 2021. Researchers have used MSL survey data in several studies investigating the outcomes of college students' participation in co-curricular activities, including students' sense of belonging (Soria et al., 2013, 2019b; Soria & Roberts, 2021). Common psychometric concerns related to self-reported data (i.e., social desirability, halo effect, and item format) are not problematic in the MSL survey (Dugan, 2015). Several changes have also been made over time to improve the psychometric properties of the instrument, including removing and rephrasing individual items and constructs (Dugan, 2015).

In the survey, students were asked to share information about whether they have ever been involved in any student groups or organizations during college (yes/no). In the original pre-matched sample (n = 49,307),

64.0% of students had participated in at least one student organization and 36.0% had not participated in at least one student organization. Given that the sample had more students in the "treatment" condition than the "control" condition, the final sample only included 21,036 students (50 percent of whom had participated and 50 percent of whom had not participated in at least one student organization).

Sample

The final sample described in Table 7.1 primarily included cisgender women (63.2 percent), white students (61.4 percent), continuing-generation students (61.9 percent), non-transfer students (76.7 percent), middle-class students (42.9 percent), and students who were enrolled full-time (95.6 percent). Most respondents also attended larger institutions (10,000+ enrollment, 65.3 percent), private institutions (57.9 percent), and doctoral institutions (59.8 percent). The limited diversity in the sample should be noted by those who are seeking to generalize the results of the present study to students on their own campuses.

Researchers' Positionality

I (Krista) am a white, working-class, disabled, first-generation college student from a rural community. I attended a small liberal arts university in a major metropolitan area and often struggled to feel a genuine sense of belonging as a rural, working-class, first-generation student, although my white privilege, hidden disability, and academic capital enabled me to "pass" amid sometimes debilitating imposter syndrome. The feeling of not belonging in higher education persists. I am dedicated to helping marginalized, minoritized, and systemically excluded students to feel valued in higher education and I have spent a considerable amount of time researching programs and practices to support students' sense of belonging. Those characteristics, experiences, and perspectives influenced my interest in pursuing this study, my ethic of care for supporting students in higher education, and how I approached and conceptualized the research design.

I (Erin) am a white female who grew up in an upper middle-class suburban community in the Midwest. Education, in general, and attending

Table 7.1 Descriptive Information for Participants

	n	%
Race/Ethnicity		
Middle Eastern or Northern African	209	1.0
African American or Black	1,147	5.5
American Indian or Alaska Native	65	0.3
Asian American	1,800	8.6
Native Hawaiian or Pacific Islander	16	0.1
Latinx or Hispanic	1,829	8.7
Multiracial	2,485	11.8
White	12,923	61.4
Race Not Listed	562	2.6
Social Class		
Low-income or poor	2,298	10.9
Working-class	4,506	21.4
Middle-class	9,033	42.9
Upper professional or upper middle-class	4,774	22.8
Wealthy	425	2.0
Sexual Orientation		
Asexual	874	4.2
Bisexual	1,994	9.5
Gay	336	1.6
Lesbian	318	1.5
Heterosexual	15,267	72.6
Pansexual	280	1.3
Queer	190	0.9
Questioning or unsure	460	2.2
Preferred response not listed	347	1.6
Multiple categories selected	970	4.6
Gender		
Man	7,041	33.5
Woman	13,286	63.2
Transgender	85	0.4
Genderqueer, gender non-conforming, or non-binary	370	1.8
Questioning or unsure	170	0.8
Preferred gender not listed in the survey	84	034
Parental Education		
Continuing-generation	13,027	61.9
First-generation	8,009	38.1

(*Continued*)

Table 7.1 (Continued)

	n	%
Disability		
Deaf or hard of hearing	106	0.5
Blind or visual impairment	194	0.9
Speech or language condition	27	0.1
Learning disability	103	0.4
Physical or musculoskeletal (e.g., multiple sclerosis)	46	0.2
Attention deficit disorder or attention deficit hyperactivity disorder	398	1.9
Psychiatric or psychological condition	1,023	4.9
Neurological condition (e.g., brain injury, stroke)	49	0.2
Medical (e.g., diabetes, severe asthma)	117	0.2
Does not have a disability	16,811	79.9
Disability not listed	155	0.7
Multiple disabilities	2,007	9.5
Transfer Status		
Non-transfer	16,136	76.7
Transfer	4,900	23.3
Enrollment Status		
Full-time	20,100	95.6
Part-time	936	4.4
Class Level		
First Year	6,001	28.5
Second Year	4,726	22.5
Third Year	5,060	24.1
Fourth Year and Beyond	5,249	24.9
Employment		
Working in an off-campus job unaffiliated with school	7,309	34.7
Working in an on campus job	3,247	15.4
Residence		
Off-campus with partner, spouse, and/or children	1,706	8.1
Off-campus with parent/guardian or other relative	6,145	29.2
Other off-campus home, apartment, or room	5,410	25.7
College/university residence hall	6,419	30.5
Other on campus student housing	924	4.4
Fraternity or sorority house	273	1.3
Other residence	159	0.8

(*Continued*)

Table 7.1 (Continued)

	n	%
Academic Majors		
Natural sciences	2,828	13.4
Science, technology, engineering, or mathematics	3,333	15.7
Business or communications	3,846	18.3
Health-related	2,113	10.0
Education	1,236	5.9
Humanities	723	8.3
Pre-professional	664	3.2
Social sciences	3,336	15.8
Undeclared or other	2,057	9.6
Carnegie Classification		
Baccalaureate	1,502	7.1
Master's colleges and universities: small and medium programs	1,174	5.6
Master's colleges and universities: larger programs	5,782	27.5
Doctoral/professional universities	2,873	13.7
Doctoral universities: High research activity	3.123	14.8
Doctoral universities: Very high research activity	6,582	31.3
Institutional Size		
Under 4,999	3,859	18.3
5,000 to 9,999	3,437	16.3
10,000 to 19,999	7,317	34.8
20,000+	6,423	30.5
Control		
Public	12,173	57.9
Private	8,863	42.1

college was prioritized throughout my life by the many educators in my family. I have spent most of my career in higher education administration with roles in career services, advising, and admissions where I supported students from a variety of backgrounds. Having worked at two Jesuit institutions, a guiding principle in my work is a Jesuit value, cura personalis, which translates to care for the whole person. In my work at the university, cura personalis guided my interactions with students, in and out of the classroom, and influenced the recommendations I made to admissions and advising policy. I am pursuing research in the attitudes and behaviors associated with the sense ofbelonging individuals feel toward an organization.

I (Justin) am a white male, third-generation college student who grew up and currently lives in a suburban, Rocky Mountain town. Both of my parents were government employees, with my mother being a public-school educator. I have been interested in human performance for over twenty-five years, the genesis of which is derived from working with athletes. My current area of inquiry is trust and belonging in public sector organizations and the resulting implications on skill development and performance indicators in the workplace.

Data Analysis

We utilized propensity score matching techniques using the "MatchIt" package in R (Ho et al., 2021) to match students in the "treatment" condition (students who had participated in at least one student organization) with those in the "control" condition (students who did not participate in at least one student organization) using covariates. We selected the following covariates because of the potential for their influence on students' decisions, access, or ability to participate in at least one student organization: institutional Carnegie classification (e.g., doctoral universities, high research activity), institutional size, and control (public or private); transfer status, enrollment status (full-time or part-time), academic major, and academic level (e.g., first-year); students' employment working in an off- or on campus position; and students' age, gender, race or ethnicity, level of parents' or guardians' education, residence (e.g., living off-campus), sexual orientation, social class, and disability status.

We began by using binary logistic regression to compute individual propensity scores: the estimated probability that students participated in a student organization. Next, we used one-to-one nearest neighbor matching without replacement, meaning that each student who had participated in at least one student organization was matched to a student with the most similar estimated propensity score who did not participate in at least one student organization. After conducting the analyses, we examined whether the matching procedures balanced the distribution of variables in both the treatment and control groups, and we determined that we decreased bias by constructing similar groups based upon the covariates we used in our analysis.

Next, we developed two factors from three survey items measuring students' sense of belonging and six survey items measuring students' perception of campus climate. For the sense of belonging scale, students indicated their agreement (1 = strongly disagree to 5 = strongly agree) to the items, "I feel valued as a person at this school," "I feel accepted as a part of the campus community," and "I feel I belong on this campus." For the measure of campus climate, students indicated their agreement (1 = strongly disagree to 5 = strongly agree) to the items, "I feel there is a general atmosphere of prejudice among students," "I have encountered discrimination attending this institution," "I would describe the environment on campus as negative/hostile," "faculty have discriminated against people like me," "other students have discriminated against people like me," and "staff members have discriminated against people like me." We used the "lavaan" package in R (Rosseel, 2012) to create a confirmatory factor analysis on the nine survey items, and the factorial model had good fit (CFI = 0.902, TLI = 0.904, RMSEA = 0.079, SRMR = .069; Kline, 2015). The sense of belonging factor ($\alpha = .873$, $\Omega = 0.842$) and the campus climate factor ($\alpha = .900$, $\Omega = 0.880$) had good internal consistency, which was congruent with other research (Dugan et al., 2012; Soria & Roberts, 2021).

In our last steps, we analyzed the significant differences in sense of belonging between students who did and did not participate in a student organization conditional on students' race/ethnicity, social class, sexual orientation, gender, first-generation status, and disability. We used ordinary least squares regression to run our final analyses, included the campus climate variable as a control measure, and separated the output by students' demographic characteristics.

Key Findings

The results of the analyses suggested that participation in a student organization was associated with some, but not all, students' sense of belonging by their race/ethnicity. Specifically, African American or Black, Asian, Latinx or Hispanic, multiracial, and white students who participated in student organizations had a significantly ($p < 0.05$) higher sense of belonging compared to their matched group of peers who did not participate in a student organization ($\beta = 0.057$, $\beta = 0.116$, $\beta = 0.073$, $\beta = 0.122$, and $\beta = 0.119$, respectively; Table 7.2). Those effects held while

Table 7.2 Regression Results for Students' Sense of Belonging

	β	*95% CI (β)*	
Race/Ethnicity			
Middle Eastern or Northern African	0.111	–0.023	0.245
African American or Black	0.057*	0.002	0.114
American Indian or Alaska Native	-0.064	–0.298	0.170
Asian American	0.116***	0.071	0.161
Native Hawaiian or Pacific Islander	0.092	–0.360	0.544
Latinx or Hispanic	0.073***	0.030	0.116
Multiracial	0.122***	0.085	0.159
White	0.119***	0.103	0.135
Race Not Listed	0.066	–0.015	0.147
Social Class			
Low-income or poor	0.100***	0.061	0.139
Working-class	0.117***	0.089	0.145
Middle-class	0.095***	0.075	0.115
Upper professional or upper middle-class	0.116***	0.089	0.143
Wealthy	0.121*	0.029	0.213
Sexual Orientation			
Asexual	0.064*	0.002	0.130
Bisexual	0.112***	0.070	0.154
Gay	0.100*	0.004	0.204
Lesbian	0.102*	0.003	0.207
Heterosexual	0.108***	0.093	0.123
Pansexual	0.280***	0.171	0.389
Queer	0.099*	0.016	0.304
Questioning or unsure	0.125*	0.038	0.212
Preferred response not listed	0.101*	0.001	0.203
Multiple categories selected	0.149*	0.089	0.209
Gender			
Man	0.073***	0.050	0.096
Woman	0.127***	0.111	0.143
Transgender	0.148*	0.049	0.345
Genderqueer, gender non-conforming, or non-binary	0.157***	0.063	0.251
Questioning or unsure	0.149***	0.021	0.297
Preferred gender not listed in the survey	0.192***	0.007	0.391

(Continued)

Table 7.2 (Continued)

	β	95% CI (β)	
Parental Education			
Continuing-generation	0.117***	0.101	0.133
First-generation	0.092***	0.071	0.113
Disability			
Deaf or hard of hearing	0.063	–0.124	0.250
Blind or visual impairment	0.134*	0.004	0.264
Speech or language condition	0.338	–0.023	0.699
Learning disability	0.213*	0.031	0.395
Physical or musculoskeletal (e.g., multiple sclerosis)	0.019	–0.281	0.319
Attention deficit disorder or attention deficit hyperactivity disorder	0.047	–0.043	0.137
Psychiatric or psychological condition	0.183***	0.126	0.240
Neurological condition (e.g., brain injury, stroke)	0.146	–0.119	0.411
Medical (e.g., diabetes, severe asthma)	0.258**	0.083	0.433
Does not have a disability	0.102***	0.088	0.116
Disability not listed	0.013	–0.135	0.161
Multiple disabilities	0.129***	0.091	0.167

Note. *$p < 0.05$, **$p < 0.01$, ***$p < 0.001$

controlling for students' perceptions of campus climate. There were no significant effects of participation in student organizations for Middle Eastern or Northern African, American Indian or Alaska Native, and Native Hawaiian or Pacific Islander students, in addition to students who did not report a race/ethnicity.

Further, the results suggested that participation in a student organization was positively associated with students' sense of belonging across all social classes controlling for students' perceptions of campus climate. Students who identified as low-income, working-class, middle-class, upper-middle or upper-professional middle class, and wealthy and participated in a student organization all had significantly ($p < 0.05$) higher levels of sense of belonging compared to their matched peers who did not participate in a student organization ($\beta = 0.100$, $\beta = 0.117$, $\beta = 0.095$, $\beta = 0.116$, and $\beta = 0.121$, respectively).

The effects of participating in student organizations were also similar across students with different sexual orientations. Asexual, bisexual, gay, lesbian, heterosexual, pansexual, queer, and questioning students, along with those who had a response not listed and those who selected multiple options, had a significantly ($p < 0.05$) higher sense of belonging when they participated in student organizations compared to their matched group of peers who did not participate in at least one student organization (β = 0.064, β = 0.112, β = 0.100, β = 0.102, β = 0.108, β = 0.280, β = 0.099, β = 0.125, β = 0.101, and β = 0.149, respectively).

Similarly, among all gender groups—cisgender men, cisgender women, questioning students, transgender students, students without a preferred gender response listed, and genderqueer, gender non-confirming, or non-binary students—those who participated in a student organization had a significantly ($p < 0.05$) higher sense of belonging compared to their matched group of peers who did not participate in a student organization (β = 0.073, β = 0.127, β = 0.149, β = 0.148, β = 0.192, and β = 0.157, respectively). All the aforementioned effects held while controlling for students' perceptions of campus climate.

The effects of participating in at least one student organization were also positive and significant ($p < 0.05$) among continuing-generation students and first-generation students (β = 0.117 and β = 0.092, respectively). Finally, with regard to disability, the following groups of students who participated in at least one student organization had a significantly ($p < 0.05$) higher sense of belonging compared to a matched group who did not participate in a student organization: students without a disability, students who are blind or have visual

impairments, students with a learning disability, students with a psychiatric or psychological disability, students with a chronic illness or medical-related disability, and students with multiple disabilities (β = 0.102, β = 0.134, β = 0.213, β = 0.183, β = 0.258, and β = 0.129, respectively). Those effects held controlling for students' perceptions of campus climate. There were no effects of participating in a student organization among the following students: students who are deaf or hard of hearing, students with speech or language disabilities, students with physical disabilities, students with attention deficit disorder or attention deficit hyperactivity disorder, students with neurological disorders or disabilities, and students who do not have their disability listed.

Discussion and Recommendations

The results of the study suggest that the effects of students' participation in at least one student organization are significant and positive for students' sense of belonging across students' social class, sexual orientation, gender, or first-generation status; however, they were not statistically significant across students' race/ethnicity or types of disability. While involvement matters for students, there are conditional effects on students' sense of belonging that suggest that "what works" for some students will not necessarily work for all students. Notably, some of the student groups who did not experience the effects of a higher sense of belonging from participation in a student organization tended to have smaller sample sizes, so it may be the case that the power was reduced in those cases (Button et al., 2013). Nevertheless, a recommendation for additional research is the further exploration of whether participation in student organizations is likely to support all students equitably.

The present study was limited in its application of Astin's (1993) input-environment-output theory because we only measured whether students participated in a student organization (yes/no) and not their full level of psychological or physical involvement or engagement (Strayhorn, 2019), which also matters in predicting students' outcomes. Additionally, we did not measure the extent to which students' involvement helped them to develop meaningful relationships and allowed them to be their authentic selves, which are important in boosting students' sense of belonging (Vaccaro & Newman, 2016).

As it relates to prospective policies and practices in higher education, the results by and large suggest that many—but not all—college students who participate in at least one student organization may experience a significantly higher level of belonging compared to a matched group of peers who did not participate in at least one student organization. Students from marginalized, minoritized, and systemically excluded backgrounds are likely—but not guaranteed—to benefit from an enhanced sense of belonging when they participate in at least one student organization over the course of their academic career. While we are encouraged by the results, it is important for practitioners to consider some of the potential barriers to students' participation in student groups, clubs, or organizations. Students may experience challenges in joining student organizations due to potential membership expenses or scheduling conflicts with work or family responsibilities. Therefore, practitioners should expand access to student organization participation through scholarships or fee waivers. We also encourage student leaders to avoid scheduling organization meetings or events during times that students may typically be employed or spending time with families and to offer flexible participation opportunities. Practitioners and student leaders who create conditions for group members to build meaningful connections with each other and validate students' authentic selves are likely to reap the greatest gains in students' sense of belonging (Vaccaro & Newman, 2016).

Conclusion

While students' participation in at least one student organization may be associated with increases in sense of belonging for many students, the results of participation were not universal among all students in our sample. We encourage researchers, practitioners, and student leaders to explore the means through which participation in student organizations may support or suppress students' sense of belonging, create more accessible and equitable opportunities for students to become involved in student organizations, and foster conditions in student organizations to meaningfully validate students' identities.

References

Astin, A. W. (1993). *What matters in college: Four critical years revisited.* Jossey-Bass.

Bettencourt, G. M. (2021). "I belong because it wasn't made for me": Understanding working- class students' sense of belonging on campus. *Journal of Higher Education, 92*(5), 760–783. https://doi.org/10.1080/00221546.2021.1872288

Blakmon, Z. R., O'Hara, R. M., & Viars, J. W. (2020). Microaggressions, sense of belonging, and sexual identity in the residential environment. *Journal of College and University Student Housing, 46*(3), 46–59.

BrckaLorenz, A., Duran, A., Fassett, K., & Palmer, D. (2021). The within-group differences in LGBQ+ college students' belongingness, institutional commitment, and outness. *Journal of Diversity in Higher Education, 14*(1), 135–146. https://doi.org/10.1037/dhe0000135

Button, K. S., Ioannidis, J. P. A., Mokryzs, C., Nosek, B. A., Flint, J., Robinson, E. S. J., & Munafó, M. R. (2013). Power failure: Why small sample size undermines the reliability of neuroscience. *Nature Reviews Neuroscience, 14*, 365–376. https://doi.org/10.1038/nrn3475

Davis, G. M., Hanzsek-Brill, M. B., Petzold, M. C., & Robinson, D. H. (2019). Students' sense of belonging: The development of a predictive retention model. *Journal of the Scholarship of Teaching and Learning, 19*(1), 117–127. https://doi.org/10.14434/josotl.v19i1.26787

Dugan, J. P. (2015). The measurement of socially responsible leadership: Considerations in establishing psychometric rigor. *Educational, Cultural, and Psychological Studies, 12*, 23–42. https://doi.org/10.7358/ecps-2015-012-duga

Dugan, J. P., Kusel, M. L., & Simounet, D. M. (2012). Transgender college students: An exploratory study of perceptions, engagement, and educational outcomes. Journal of College Student Development, 53(5), 719-736.

Duran, A., Dahl, L. S., Stipeck, C., & Mayhew, M. J. (2020). A critical quantitative analysis of students' sense of belonging: Perspectives on race, generation status, and collegiate environments. *Journal of College Student Development, 61*(2), 133–153. http://doi.org/10.1353/csd.2020.0014

Gopalan, M., & Brady, S. T. (2020). College students' sense of belonging: A national perspective. *Educational Researcher, 49*(2), 134–137. https://doi.org/10.3102/0013189X1989762

Ho, D., Imai, K., King, G., Stuart, E., Whitworth, A., & Greifer, N. (2021). *Package 'MatchIt.'* https://cran.r-project.org/web/packages/MatchIt/MatchIt.pdf

Hoffman, M., Richmond, J., Morrow, J., & Salomone, K. (2002). Investigating "sense of belonging" in first-year college students. *Journal of College Student Retention: Research, Theory & Practice, 4*(3), 227–256. http://dx.doi.org/10.2190/ DRYC-CXQ9- JQ8V-HT4V

Hurst, A. L. (2012). *College and the working class: What it takes to make it.* Sense.

Johnson, D. R., Soldner, M., Leonard, J. B., Alvarez, P., Inkelas, K. K., Rowan-Kenyon, H. T., & Longerbeam, S. D. (2007). Examining sense of belonging among first-year undergraduates from different racial/ethnic groups. *Journal of College Student Development, 48*(5), 525–542. https://doi.org/10.1353/csd.2007.0054.

Kline, R. B. (2015). *Principles and practice of structural equation modeling.* Guilford.

Lewis, J. A., Mendenhall, R., Ojiemwe, A., Thomas, M., Riopelle, C., Harwood, S. A., & Huntt, M. B. (2021). Racial microaggressions and sense of belonging at a historically White university. *American Behavioral Scientist*, 65(8), 1049–1071. https://doi.org /10 .1177 /0002764219859613

Museus, S. D., & Chang, T.-H. (2021). The impact of campus environments on sense of belonging for first-generation college students. *Journal of College Student Development, 62*(3), 367–372.

Museus, S. D., & Maramba, D. C. (2011). The impact of culture on Filipino American students' sense of belonging. *The Review of Higher Education, 34*(2), 231–258. https://doi.org/10.1353/rhe.2010.0022.

Museus, S. D., Yi, V., & Saelua, N. (2017). The impact of culturally engaging campus environments on sense of belonging. *The Review of Higher Education*, *40*(2), 187–215. https://doi.org/10.1353/rhe.2017.0001.

Parker, E. T., III (2021). Campus climate perceptions and sense of belonging for LGBTQ students: A Canadian case study. *Journal of College Student Development*, *62*(2), 248–253. https://doi.org/10.1353/csd.2021.0019.

Rodriguez, S. L., & Blaney, J. M. (2021). "We're the unicorns in STEM": Understanding how academic and social experiences influence sense of belonging for Latina undergraduate students. *Journal of Diversity in Higher Education*, *14*(3), 441–455. https://doi.org/10.1037/dhe0000176

Rosseel, Y. (2012). lavaan: An R package for structural equation modeling. *Journal of Statistical Software*, *48*(2), 1–36. https://doi.org/10.18637/jss .v048.i02

Soria, K. M. (2015). *Welcoming blue collar scholars into the ivory tower: Developing class- conscious strategies for students' success.* National Resource Center for the First-Year Experience and Students in Transition.

Soria, K. M. (Ed.). (2018). *Evaluating campus climate at U.S. research universities: Opportunities for diversity and inclusion*. Palgrave Macmillan. https://doi.org/10.1007/978-3-319-94836-2

Soria, K. M. (2021). *Supporting undergraduate students with disabilities: A focus on campus climate and sense of belonging*. National Center for College Students with Disabilities.

Soria, K. M., & Alkire, D. B. (2015). Elevating Native American college students' sense of belonging in higher education. *Developments Journal*, *13*(3). https://developments.myacpa.org/elevating-native-american -college-students-sense-of- belonging-in-higher-education/

Soria, K. M., & Bultmann, M. (2014). Advising scholars from blue collar backgrounds: Supporting working-class students' success in higher education. *NACADA Journal, 34*(2), 51–62. https://doi.org/10.12930/NACADA-13-017

Soria, K. M., Fink, A., Lepkowski, C. C., & Snyder, L. (2013). Undergraduate student leadership and social change. *Journal of College and Character, 14*(3), 241–252. https://doi.org/10.1515/jcc- 2013-0031

Soria, K. M., & Mitchell, T. D. (2015). Learning communities: Foundations for first-year students' development of pluralistic outcomes. *Learning Communities Research and Practice, 3*(2), 1–21.

Soria, K. M., & Roberts, B. J. (2021). The benefits of living on campus for first-generation students' belonging, perceptions of campus climate, and resilience. *Journal of First- Generation Student Success, 1*(2), 111–126. https://doi.org/10.1080/26906015.2021.1926373

Soria, K. M., & Stebleton, M. J. (2012). First-generation students' academic engagement and retention. *Teaching in Higher Education, 17*(6), 1–13. https://doi.org/10.1080/13562517.2012.666735

Soria, K. M., & Stebleton, M. J. (2013). Social capital, academic engagement, and sense of belonging among working-class college students. *College Student Affairs Journal, 31*(2), 139–153.

Soria, K. M., Stebleton, M. J., & Huesman, R. L. (2013–2014). Class counts: Exploring differences in academic and social integration between working-class and middle/upper- class students at large, public research universities. *Journal of College Student Retention: Research, Theory, and Practice, 15*(2), 215–242. https://doi.org/10.2190%2FCS.15.2.e

Soria, K. M., Werner, L., Chandiramani, N., Day, M., & Asmundson, A. (2019a). Co-curricular engagement as catalysts toward students' leadership development and multicultural competence. *Journal of Student Affairs Research and Practice, 56*(2), 207–220. https://doi.org/10.1080/19496591.2018.1519439

Soria, K. M., Werner, L., & Nath, C. (2019b). Leadership experiences and perspective taking among college students. *Journal of Student Affairs Research and Practice, 56*(2), 138–152. https://doi.org/10.1080/19496591.2018.1490309

Stebleton, M. J., Soria, K. M., & Huesman, R. L. (2014). Recent immigrant students at research universities: The relationship between campus climate and sense of belonging. *Journal of College Student Development, 55*(2), 196–202. https://doi.org/10.1353/csd.2014.0019

Stephens, N., Hamedani, M., & Destin, M. (2014). Closing the social-class achievement gap: A difference-education intervention improves first-generation students' academic performance and all students' college transition. *Psychological Science, 25*, 943–953. https://doi.org/10.1177%2F0956797613518349

Strayhorn, T. L. (2008a). Fittin' in: Do diverse interactions with peers affect sense of belonging for Black men at predominantly White institutions? *NASPA Journal*, *45*(4), 501–527. https://doi.org/10.2202/1949-6605.2009

Strayhorn, T. L. (2008b). Sentido de pertenencia: A hierarchical analysis predicting sense of belonging among Latino college students. *Journal of Hispanic Higher Education*, *7*(4), 301–320. https://doi.org/10.1177/1538192708320474

Strayhorn, T. L. (2019). *College students' sense of belonging: A key to educational success for all students* (2nd ed.). Routledge. https://doi.org/10.4324/9781315297293

Tachine, A. R., Cabrera, N. L., & Yellow Bird, E. (2017). Home away from home: Native American students' sense of belonging during their first year of college. *The Journal of Higher Education*, *88*(5), 785–807. https://doi.org/10.1080/00221546.2016.1257322

Taylor, J. A., Macke, C., Ozaki, R., Lindsey, M., & Anderson, A. (2022). The intersection of sense of belonging and financial hardship among university students. *Re-Envisioning the Social Work Profession, Education, and Practice*, *22*(2), 454–474. https://doi.org/10.18060/24963

Vaccaro, A., & Newman, B. M. (2016). Development of a sense of belonging for privileged and minoritized students: An emergent model. *Journal of College Student Development*, *57*(8), 925–942. https://doi.org/10.1353/csd.2016.0091.

Vaccaro, A., & Newman, B. M. (2017). A sense of belonging through the eyes of first-year LGBPQ students. *Journal of Student Affairs Research and Practice*, *54*(2), 137–149. https://doi.org/10.1080/19496591.2016.1211533

Villalpando, O., & Solórzano, D. G. (2005). The role of culture in college preparation programs: A review of the research literature. In w. G. Tierney, Z. B. Corwin, & J. E. Colyar (Eds.), *Preparing for college: Nine elements of effective outreach* (pp. 13–28). State University of New York Press.

Yosso, T. J. (2005). Whose culture has capital? A critical race theory discussion of community cultural wealth. *Race, Ethnicity, and Education*, *8*(1), 69–91. https://doi.org/10.1080/1361332052000341006

8

The Trifecta

The WHOLE Student Experience, Sense of Belonging, and Historically Black Colleges and Universities (HBCUs)

Morris Thomas and Cindy Philpot

Chapter Outline

> Having a sense of belonging for students is as essential as shelter for the unhoused on a frigid winter's night; it can be the determining factor in whether a student persists, thrives, and ultimately achieves their desired outcomes.
>
> —Dr. Morris Thomas

Introduction

In higher education, cultivating students' sense of belonging is essential for supporting academic well-being, personal growth, and success (Strayhorn, 2019). More attention to the notion of belonging has become the focus of practitioners and scholars as institutions strive to create inclusive and engaging learning environments. This chapter discusses the powerful intersection between student involvement and sense of belonging in light of the unique role that Historically Black Colleges and Universities (HBCUs) play in nurturing connections and community among the students they serve (Harrison & Thomas, 2021).

As Strayhorn (2019) posits, a sense of belonging is a basic human need that is essential for student success and well-being, particularly in educational contexts. When students feel like they belong, they are more likely to be engaged, motivated, and confident in their abilities, leading to improved academic outcomes and increased persistence and retention. However, despite the growing literature and attention given to the sense of belonging, more information is needed about student experiences at HBCUs. Indeed, HBCUs have a long history of nurturing community, connectedness, and racial pride among HBCU faculty, staff, and students (Palmer & Gasman, 2008). Therefore, this chapter does just that by providing further exploration of a sense of belonging for college students attending HBCUs.

To explore the role of student involvement in fostering a sense of belonging, this chapter introduces the WHOLE Experience framework, which considers five components: Welcoming, Holistic, Open, Liberating, and Empowering. Student involvement is central to this framework, as participation in campus activities, organizations, and leadership roles can significantly contribute to students feeling more connected to their institution (Burmicky et al., 2022). By examining each element of the framework and its supporting research, the chapter offers valuable insights into effective strategies for promoting inclusion and enhancing the overall student experience. Central to this discussion is the unique role that HBCUs play in providing "The WHOLE Experience." Indeed, HBCUs have an extensive history of fostering a sense of community and pride among HBCU students, faculty, and staff by way of nurturing and affirming their cultural identity (Palmer & Gasman, 2008). Involvement in student organizations, Greek life, and leadership opportunities at HBCUs often acts as a catalyst for students' deeper engagement with both their peers and the institution itself, further reinforcing their sense of belonging.

Ultimately, this chapter aims to contribute to the growing conversation around the importance of student involvement in enhancing a sense of belonging in higher education by focusing on the transformative power of involvement, highlighting the exemplary practices of HBCUs. By exploring the trifecta of the WHOLE Experience, sense of belonging, and student involvement at HBCUs, the chapter offers practical insights and strategies for creating learning environments that empower students to thrive academically, socially, and personally. As institutions seek to cultivate more inclusive and equitable communities, this chapter serves as a valuable resource for scholars, researchers, practitioners, and policymakers committed to fostering conditions that boost a sense of belonging through student involvement and, consequently, promote student success and well-being in higher education.

Literature Review

Creating inclusive and engaging learning experiences is crucial for fostering academic success, involvement, and a sense of belonging among diverse learners (Thomas & Thomas, 2023). This literature review explores the WEF, which emphasizes the importance of creating learning environments that are Welcoming, Holistic, Open, Liberating, and Empowering. Examining each element of the framework and supporting research, insights are provided for effective strategies to promote inclusion and enhance the overall learning experience, especially at HBCUs.

Welcoming

Welcoming learning environments are essential for engaging learners and fostering community (Thomas & Thomas, 2023). Harrison and Thomas (2021) introduce the Enhance(d) Learning Model (ELM), which highlights the importance of positively engaging learners in three distinct ways: learner-to-instructor, learner-to-content, and learner-to-learner. Building connections between *the learner* and *what is learned* nurtures a welcoming atmosphere and promotes a positive academic experience. ELM emphasizes the connection between learners' emotional and cognitive aspects, which can significantly impact *what learners do*, reflecting dimensions of involvement. In order to foster community and promote student involvement, the notion of hospitality should be included. Hospitality traits such as enthusiasm, inclusivity, attention to detail, and helpfulness (Brotherton & Wood, 2010) are key components. Additionally, in higher education, integrating principles of andragogy aids in student involvement by focusing on students' unique needs. Andragogy has six assumptions or principles, several of which specifically provide means for better involving students, such as ensuring the experiences provided are relevant, recognizing the students' sense of self and factors that contribute to their internal motivation (Chan, 2010).

HBCUs have provided welcoming environments for their students, especially Black students who were once denied admission elsewhere due to racism and discrimination (Harrison & Thomas, 2021; Palmer & Gasman, 2008). HBCUs foster a keen sense of community and pride among faculty, staff, and students by creating a supportive and nurturing atmosphere that acknowledges and celebrates African American culture, history, and experiences (Strayhorn, 2023). This welcoming environment is critical for student involvement and sense of belonging, as it provides a foundation for students to engage fully in campus life (Burmicky et al., 2022).

Holistic

A holistic approach to learning considers the "whole" is greater than the sum of its parts. For instance, the student experience is shaped by the time and energy that students devote to academic and social activities (i.e., involvement), plus their feelings about those experiences, namely sense of belonging (Strayhorn, 2019). Moreover, Fink (2005) emphasizes the importance of considering situational factors, such as students' life situations, prior knowledge, goals, and expectations, when designing transformative learning experiences. Holistic approaches, then, would take into account a blend of these points when working with students.

To appreciate the whole student and his/her situational backgrounds, educators need proven strategies for getting to know them; two of these are *Network* and *Connect* according to ELM (Harrison & Thomas, 2021). Networking facilitates relationships between students, staff, and peers, in ways that produce knowledge acquisition through engagement (Thomas & Thomas, 2023). *Connect* recognizes the importance of human interaction and communication in creating opportunities for instructors to form appropriate emotional bonds with students (Thomas et al., 2017). Networking, connections, and bonds enable a holistic approach that improves student experiences.

HBCUs have long since adopted a holistic approach to education, focusing on the emotional, intellectual, personal, social, and spiritual development of students (Williams et al., 2004). Consequently, they provide a wide range of academic and extracurricular activities that cater to the diverse interests and needs of their students. These include, without limits: campus traditions (e.g., Royal Court), gospel choirs, Black fraternities and sororities, to name a few. Ultimately, deep involvement in such race-conscious activities can foster HBCU students' sense of belonging and personal growth (Williams et al., 2004).

Open

Openness is defined as transparency and the freedom to share ideas without fear of harm or humiliation (Baker lll, 2017). Honest communication between staff and students creates healthy campus conditions that facilitate academic learning, involvement, and success. Students with frequent open exchanges with staff and peers feel safe and supported to participate in campus activities, persist, and thrive in college. For example, students who regularly engage in open discussions with instructors during office hours or peer study groups are more likely to feel comfortable asking questions, joining extracurricular activities, and maintaining good academic standing throughout college. These campus involvement experiences foster a sense of belonging, which boosts academic success.

Incorporating intentional practices that encourage open communication is crucial for improving student experiences and fostering inclusive environments. Inclusive spaces provide access, power sharing, and voice for participants (Özturgut, 2017). By intentionally including opportunities for students and practitioners to pause, provide feedback, and engage in self-reflection (Gay, 2018), educators can support the improvement of the overall experience while promoting open, equitable, and nurturing environments that encourage campus involvement and make sense of belonging possible.

A long line of studies shows that faculty and staff at HBCUs encourage students to openly express their opinions and ideas freely (Harrison & Thomas, 2021). They serve as safe spaces where students can explore their identities, discuss social and political issues, and engage in critical thinking and self-reflection without fear of judgment (Harrison & Thomas, 2021). This open environment found on HBCU campuses fosters student involvement and creates a sense of belonging, as it allows students to fully express themselves and engage in meaningful dialogue with peers and faculty (Johnson & Winfield, 2022).

Liberating

Liberating is defined as the act of freeing a person, thing, or place from a situation, especially one that's duly restrictive. Liberating educational environments are celebrative, flexible, and adaptable. For example, a liberating educational environment might allow students to choose their own research topic, work collaboratively on projects, and present their findings through various mediums such as videos, podcasts, or interactive websites, rather than being limited to traditional essays or exams. Traditional academic environments often lack the necessary flexibility to accommodate the diverse needs of learners (Thomas & Thomas, 2023) such as those over the age of twenty-five, working students, parents, first-generation college students, and Pell Grant-eligible students (Yavorski, 2019). Liberating can also be found through freedom of self-expression. According to Johnson and McGowan (2017) HBCUs provide spaces where Black students can fully express themselves without the burden of code-switching. Being able to fully express oneself lends to an increased sense of belonging and willingness to become an involved student.

Universal Design for Learning (UDL) provides a framework for creating flexible, adaptable, and liberating learning environments (Al-Azawei et al., 2016). UDL recommends providing students with multiple means of engagement, expression, and representation. For example, instructors can provide course materials in various formats (e.g., written, multimedia) to cater to different learning preferences. Additionally, allowing students to engage in written, verbal, or electronic formats can promote multiple means of engagement and expression. This liberation is manifested at HBCUs through curriculum choices, teaching methods, and campus culture that affirm and empower Black students (Williams et al., 2021).At their core, HBCUs have served as liberating spaces for students and their communities. HBCUs were founded to offer educational opportunities to African American students—the offspring of formerly enslaved people who were *literally unfree* due to the pains of slavery, segregation, and racism (Harrison & Thomas, 2021). By encouraging student involvement on campus and belonging, HBCUs can help liberate the soul.

Empowering

An empowering learning environment provides opportunities for achieving students desired outcomes. Empowerment refers to increasing the capacity of individuals or groups to make choices about what they want and to transform those choices into desired actions and outcomes (Zimmerman, 2000). The empowerment component of the WEF is closely connected to student involvement, as engaged students are more likely to develop leadership skills and a sense of agency (Strayhorn, 2019).

Creating an environment that fosters a sense of belonging is crucial for empowering learners. Strayhorn (2020) defines a sense of belonging as a student's perceived social support on campus, a feeling of connectedness, and the experience of mattering or feeling cared about, accepted, respected, valued, and important to the group. One strategy for empowering students is diversifying representation in course content to help learners feel like they belong (Lee & Fogle, 2020). Campus involvement also helps build a strong community among students, thereby enhancing engagement, learning, and a satisfying experience (Schwitzer et al., 1999). Studies have shown that the more time and effort students invest in the academic and social opportunities available in a learning environment, the more enhanced their academic achievement, personal growth, satisfaction, and persistence will be (Chu, 2016). Johnson and Winfield (2022) found that racial isolation and positive interaction with HBCU students were the main motivations for participants to select an HBCU. Similarly, Williams et al. (2021) reported that many Black students who had selected to attend a predominantly white institution (PWI) did not feel accepted, highlighting the unique role HBCUs play in creating an affirming and empowering environment for Black students.

Of all their strengths, scholars have documented that HBCUs boast empowering conditions their students need to succeed academically and personally. They provide supportive and nurturing environments that foster a sense of belonging among students (Williams et al., 2021). Additionally, HBCUs have a strong tradition of community engagement and service, empowering their students to become leaders and change agents in their communities (Williams et al., 2021).

Throughout this literature review, we have outlined how each element of the WEF relates to the environments and histories of HBCUs. HBCUs foster a keen sense of belonging among their students by providing supportive and nurturing environments that acknowledge and celebrate their culture, history, and experiences. By examining HBCUs practices and traditions, educators can gain valuable insights into how they can provide a "WHOLE" experience that facilitates conditions of a sense of belonging, ultimately promoting student success and well-being.

Purpose of the Chapter and Associated Study

The chapter and its associated study aim to investigate the interconnectedness between student involvement and sense of belonging within the unique role of HBCUs in fostering inclusive and supportive learning environments. This research explores these elements through the WEF to contribute practical insights for creating more engaging and equitable college communities, using commencement speeches by HBCU students as a primary data source.

The study associated with this chapter uses content analysis to investigate how themes, concepts, and language related to the WEF appear in commencement speeches delivered by students at HBCUs. By purposively selecting a representative sample of speeches, the study aims to reveal how HBCUs not only embody and promote the elements of the WHOLE Experience but also how these elements contribute to fostering student involvement and a strong sense of belonging. The WHOLE framework's components—Welcoming, Holistic, Open, Liberating, and Empowering—are critical in shaping environments that actively engage students, allowing them to feel valued, included, and motivated to participate in campus life.

Furthermore, this chapter seeks to amplify the voices and stories of Black students who have long been excluded from dominant narratives of higher education, demonstrating the transformative power of institutions that prioritize belonging, inclusion, and equity. The WHOLE framework is integral to understanding how HBCUs create inclusive spaces that foster deep student involvement, leading to a heightened sense of belonging. Ultimately, this chapter highlights the dynamic relationship between the institutional context of HBCUs, student involvement, and sense of belonging, offering a roadmap for creating college environments that nurture academic, social, and personal growth for all students.

The Study

Research Design

The study employs a qualitative research design, specifically utilizing content analysis as the primary research method. Content analysis is a research methodology used to effectively examine the presence of certain words, themes, or concepts within qualitative data, such as commencement speeches at HBCUs (Hsieh & Shannon, 2005). Additionally, Neuendorf (2002) asserts that content analysis is a systematic and objective approach to analyzing qualitative data, such as text or speech, to identify patterns, themes, and meanings. Thus, this was deemed an appropriate design for the chapter's study.

Sample/Participants

The study's sample included three commencement speakers from Historically Black Colleges and Universities (HBCUs): one from Bennett College, North Carolina A&T University, and Florida A&M University.

The first participant was an African American female, a senior at North Carolina A&T University at the time of her speech in 2024. She held the position of Senior Class President and delivered a commencement address that highlighted the university's strong support system, particularly the faculty's commitment to student success. Her speech emphasized the pride and unity that define the university's community and reflected on the institution's historical and academic significance.

The second participant was an African American male, a graduating senior from Florida A&M University in 2023. In his commencement speech, he focused on the resilience demonstrated by his class, pointing out how they overcame challenges such as the global pandemic and socio-political divides, all while thriving academically. His speech emphasized the unique culture at FAMU that fosters leadership, resilience, and professional growth, and he reflected on the pride of being part of the university's legacy.

The third participant was an African American female, a graduating senior from Bennett College in 2021. In her commencement speech, she reflected on how her involvement on campus as a Resident Assistant (RA) and participation in student organizations helped shape her into a leader. She highlighted the deep sense of sisterhood and community that Bennett fostered, where students from diverse backgrounds connected through shared values and experiences. Her speech emphasized how Bennett's close-knit environment provided her with the strength and confidence to succeed, both academically and personally. She expressed gratitude for the lifelong bonds she formed and how the supportive atmosphere helped her thrive.

Data Collection

The study uses purposive sampling to select a representative sample of commencement speeches delivered by students at Historically Black Colleges and Universities (HBCUs). Purposive sampling, a nonprobability sampling technique, allows researchers to deliberately choose participants based on specific characteristics, knowledge, or experiences that align with the study's objectives. In this case, speeches were chosen for their potential to provide rich insights into the culture, values, and practices of HBCUs, particularly how these institutions foster a sense of belonging and promote student success.

The sample includes three speeches, delivered by HBCU students, strategically selected to ensure diversity of perspective. This intentional selection enables a comprehensive examination of the varied experiences and perspectives of individuals deeply connected to the HBCU community. Through these lenses, the study seeks to explore how HBCUs create a supportive and empowering environment for students and how these institutions influence their graduates and the broader community.

Data Analysis

The content analysis was designed to investigate which elements of the HBCU experience, as portrayed in the commencement speeches, align with the WHOLE Experience Framework and how they foster a sense of belonging and student involvement. The speeches, which were five to seven minutes long, were sourced from YouTube. Transcripts of the speeches were downloaded for analysis. The speeches were then coded into manageable categories to identify emerging themes. The coding process was conducted using embedded software search capabilities within the transcriptions to efficiently analyze the content and discover relevant themes.

By analyzing the language used in these speeches, we can gain valuable insights into the culture, values, and messages conveyed in such talks. These speeches are rich sources of data that can provide a deeper understanding of the unique experiences, challenges, and triumphs of the HBCU community.

Commencement speeches at HBCUs hold significance for the education and empowerment of Black students and other students of color. These speeches celebrate achievements, inspire, and empower graduates, affirm cultural identity and community, address societal challenges, and preserve the legacy of HBCUs (Rasheed et al., 2017; Williams & Ashley, 2004). Commencement speakers at HBCUs often serve as role models, sharing stories of perseverance and success that demonstrate to students that they can overcome adversity and achieve their goals (Bridges et al., 2005). These messages of empowerment are especially important for Black students who may face additional barriers and discrimination (Toldson & Cooper, 2014)—pointing back to the "E" in WHOLE framework. Commencement speeches are critical to analyze because they capture the essence of the HBCU experience in one of its most notable events, which often displays the pride in one's heritage, the value of community support, and the responsibility to give back to one's community (Bridges et al., 2005).

Trustworthiness and Accuracy of Data

To ensure data quality and accuracy, we enhanced the study's trustworthiness by employing the following: (1) the establishment of clear and consistent protocols for data collection and analysis, including the development of a coding scheme that reflects the key elements of the WHOLE Experience framework and (2) the data analysis for this study is being conducted by the Director and Associate Director of the Center for Excellence in Teaching, Learning, and Assessment (CETLA) at Howard University, both of whom are currently employed at this prestigious HBCU. As researchers, we are deeply engaged in the process of reflexivity, acknowledging our positionality as members of the HBCU community. Both of us have extensive experience working with students and faculty at Howard University as well as other HBCUs, and our daily interactions with the culture and values of HBCUs inevitably shape our interpretation of the data.

Additionally, our roles as employees of an HBCU grant us a unique insider perspective, which may provide valuable insights into understanding the broader HBCU community. We have also each studied at HBCUs. However, we also recognize that our personal experiences, backgrounds, and potential biases could influence the ways in which we analyze the speeches. Therefore, we approach this study with a commitment to critical reflexivity—remaining aware of how our positionality as HBCU alumni and professionals may inform our perceptions and interpretation of the themes related to belonging, culture, and student success. By continually reflecting on these factors, we aim to ensure a balanced and objective analysis of the data while acknowledging the richness of our connection to the HBCU environment. This study used a combination of conceptual and relational analysis by quantifying and counting certain concepts' presence. The conceptual analysis included identifying word usage and frequency in the HBCU commencement speeches, while the relational analysis looked at how these concepts are connected to each other and to the overall messages within the speeches.

Key Findings

The analysis of commencement speech transcripts from Historically Black Colleges and Universities (HBCUs) reveals common themes related to the WHOLE (Welcoming, Holistic, Open, Liberating, and Empowering) framework, sense of belonging, and the unique role of HBCUs in fostering inclusive learning environments. The speeches emphasize a sense of belonging and the unique role that HBCUs play in fostering inclusive learning environments that promote personal growth and student success.

Welcoming

Across all speeches, a central theme is the welcoming atmosphere of HBCUs. Speeches from North Carolina A&T, Florida A&M, and Bennett College consistently refer to these institutions as places where students feel part of a family. Terms like "home," "community," and "family" frequently appear, describing the supportive and nurturing environment that values and celebrates each student's background and identity. For example, the speaker from Florida A&M stated, "We are one family that has shifted, molded, and shaped the lives of thousands," highlighting the class's resilience and the communal support that helped them overcome challenges like the global pandemic, fostering a strong sense of unity (FAMUTube1887, 2023). The speaker from Bennett College echoed this sentiment, emphasizing the powerful sisterhood and close bonds that form at the college, which create a safe and encouraging environment for women to grow and succeed together.

Holistic

The analysis underscores the holistic development of students, as emphasized in the speeches. Both the North Carolina A&T and Florida A&M speakers reflect on their growth—not only intellectually, but also socially and emotionally. The speeches highlight how HBCUs cater to diverse interests, fostering well-rounded individuals through a blend of academic rigor and extracurricular engagement. This support for the whole student is particularly evident in the speaker from North Carolina A&T, who mentioned the faculty's commitment to pushing students toward success, ultimately preparing them for real-world challenges.

Open

The speeches also highlight the openness fostered within HBCU environments. Speakers describe these institutions as safe spaces where students are encouraged to express themselves freely and explore their identities. Words like "authentic" and "finding your voice" were used in both speeches to communicate the sense of freedom students experienced. The speaker from Florida A&M specifically mentioned how the university helped students navigate social and political issues, encouraging open dialogue and critical thinking.

Liberating

HBCUs are portrayed as liberating spaces that equip students to challenge systemic barriers and pursue their dreams. Both the North Carolina A&T and Florida A&M speeches discuss how their institutions empowered them to push boundaries and work toward breaking down societal inequalities. The speaker from North Carolina A&T noted, "Being at A&T has been liberating—we are breaking barriers and setting the stage for future generations to follow in our footsteps," reflecting the sense of empowerment and responsibility to effect change (FAMUTube1887, 2023). The speaker from Florida A&M, in particular, stated, "FAMU has given us the tools to not just survive, but to thrive in a world that wasn't built for us," highlighting the transformative role of HBCUs in empowering students to contribute to change, despite adversity (North Carolina A&T, 2024).

Empowering

Empowerment is a recurring theme, with speakers sharing their stories of perseverance and success. The commencement addresses from these universities emphasized the importance of embracing one's talents and purpose. The Florida A&M speaker highlighted the importance of resilience and overcoming obstacles, while the North Carolina A&T speaker reflected on the pride and strength instilled in them by the university's culture. At Bennett College, a graduating senior expressed how her involvement on campus helped her grow into a leader, crediting the community's deep sense of sisterhood. She remarked, "Bennett allowed me to become the leader I never thought I could be." This empowerment and encouragement to rise above challenges resonated across all the speeches.

Sense of Belonging

The speeches repeatedly underscore the profound sense of belonging that HBCUs provide. All speakers discussed the lifelong friendships and bonds formed during their time at these institutions. They described feeling valued and supported in a community that fostered both personal and professional growth. For the speaker from North Carolina A&T, this sense of belonging was tied to the university's enduring commitment to student success, while the Florida A&M speaker spoke of the institution's role in developing leaders who remain connected to the larger HBCU community. At Bennett College, one student reflected on the strong sisterhood that shaped her experience. She shared how her involvement on campus, including serving as a Resident Assistant (RA), deepened her connection to the community, saying, "Choosing Bennett was the best decision I ever made. I never thought I'd find such a close-knit sisterhood anywhere else." This sense of belonging was pivotal in her personal growth and leadership development.

Student Involvement: Student involvement is a cornerstone of the HBCU experience, fostering a sense of belonging and personal growth.

HBCUs provide numerous opportunities for students to engage in campus life, from student organizations and leadership roles to cultural events and community service. This involvement enhances students' academic experiences and cultivates their social, emotional, and professional development. The speakers emphasized how their campus involvement shaped their journeys at HBCUs. The North Carolina A&T speaker highlighted how participating in student organizations and events helped her find her voice and celebrate her identity, while the Florida A&M speaker reflected on how campus involvement created deep connections, especially during challenging times, saying, "We are one family that has shifted, molded, and shaped the lives of thousands." Similarly, the Bennett College speaker discussed the empowering effect of involvement within the college's sisterhood, noting that it's not just about the activities but about the bonds formed that build confidence and prepare them for future challenges. These accounts illustrate that student involvement at HBCUs extends beyond academics, as it allows students to establish lifelong friendships, build networks, and grow as individuals. This supportive community values each student's unique contributions, enriching the college experience and preparing them to become active, engaged members of society.

Discussion

The content analysis of the commencement speeches delivered by students at Historically Black Colleges and Universities (HBCUs) reveals a powerful narrative of inclusion, empowerment, and belonging. Key findings highlight the unique role that HBCUs play in fostering welcoming, holistic, open, liberating, and empowering learning environments that enable students to thrive academically, socially, and personally. Content analysis also reveals a focus on the holistic development of students, with speakers discussing the intellectual, social, and emotional growth they experienced during their time at these institutions. [show don't tell] The speeches underscore the openness and freedom of expression that HBCUs encourage, creating safe spaces for students to explore their individuality, engage in critical thinking, and discuss social and political issues. As the Bennett College speaker expressed:

> I met so many wonderful people and it seems like throughout our different backgrounds in our different lives we all shared the same type of life same experience had the same mamas and grandma . . . Bennett has formed me into a leader that I never thought that I could be.

The liberating and empowering nature of the HBCU experience is highlighted, with speakers discussing the transformative power of education in breaking down barriers and challenging systemic inequalities. The North Carolina A&T graduate powerfully stated:

> I always remember that I am Black, that I have to try twice as hard, I have to never give someone a reason to push me out of this space or tell me "I don't belong or I'm not qualified or I don't fit in." Coming to an HBCU has allowed me to not have to worry about that. It's a sense of peace, I don't know if I could place anywhere else in the scope of my education.

Messages of empowerment and encouragement for the graduates are prevalent across all speech types, with speakers sharing their own stories of perseverance, resilience, and success. They urge the graduates to be bold in their ambitions, learn from their failures, and stay true to their beliefs and values.

Throughout the speeches, speakers consistently emphasize the strong sense of belonging they experienced at their respective HBCUs, attributing their personal and professional growth to the supportive and nurturing environment that these institutions provide. For instance, the Bennett student expressed:

> Bennett allowed me the opportunity to present at the prestigious Harvard University in Boston Massachusetts, at the AOCC which is the Alumni of Color Conference. This was the highlight of my college career. Freshman year I learned about myself, sophomore year I learned about my school, junior year I learned about the company I kept and my friends, and now senior year I learned that each year at Bennett actually prepared me to become a very determined woman who never gives up easily.

The findings of this study align with the growing body of literature on belonging in higher education, which highlights the fundamental importance of feeling connected, accepted, and valued within one's college community (Strayhorn, 2018). Each remarked on belonging to their respective institutions, making meaningful connections and playing active roles that they believe were inextricably tied to their attending an HBCU. [how? show don't tell] The welcoming, holistic, open, liberating, and empowering learning environments described in the HBCU commencement speeches reflect the principles of the WHOLE Experience framework introduced in this chapter, which emphasizes the importance of designing learning environments that foster inclusion and enhance the overall learning experience.

Recommendations

For Research and Theory

- Further research should be dedicated to delving into the factors that contribute to a deep sense of belonging among students at HBCUs. Both qualitative and quantitative methods should be used to fully understand the HBCU experience.
- Researchers should assess the adaptability of the WHOLE Experience framework in various educational settings, exploring how its principles can be tailored to promote inclusion and belonging in diverse institutional environments.

For Policy and Outreach

- Policymakers should recognize the unique role that Historically Black Colleges and Universities (HBCUs) play in fostering inclusion, empowerment, and belonging for African American students. Adequate funding and support should be provided to ensure the sustainability and growth of these institutions.
- Higher education institutions should collaborate with HBCUs to learn from their best practices in creating welcoming, holistic, open, liberating, and empowering learning environments, and adapt these practices to their own institutional contexts.

For Practice

- Higher education institutions should prioritize creating welcoming, holistic, open, liberating, and empowering learning environments, using the WHOLE Experience framework as a guide for designing inclusive and engaging educational experiences. Higher education institutions should prioritize the creation of welcoming, holistic, open, liberating, and empowering learning environments. The WHOLE Experience framework can guide the design of inclusive and engaging educational experiences.

- Educators should incorporate the principles of culturally responsive teaching (Gay, 2018) into their practice, acknowledging and celebrating the diverse experiences and identities of their students, and creating safe spaces for open dialogue and critical thinking.

Conclusion

In conclusion, a sense of belonging goes beyond mere social support or fitting in with others; it is a fundamental human need. It is a deep desire to feel connected, accepted, and valued within a community, and it is as essential to our well-being as the air we breathe or the food we eat. Creating a sense of belonging in higher education requires intentional efforts to create diverse, inclusive, and welcoming environments where all students feel seen, heard, and valued. When a space that provides a sense of belonging is made available, students are more likely to thrive, flourish, and succeed in their endeavors. In educational settings, a sense of belonging is particularly crucial as it leads to more engaged, motivated, and confident students. Conversely, students who feel out of place or unsupported are more likely to struggle academically and emotionally.

Commencement speeches delivered by students at HBCUs reveal a powerful narrative of inclusion, empowerment, and belonging. Speakers highlight the unique role of HBCUs in fostering welcoming, holistic, open, liberating, and empowering learning environments that enable students to thrive academically, socially, and personally. Through their stories and messages, the commencement speeches amplify the benefits of the trifecta, "The WHOLE Experience, Sense of Belonging and HBCUs." By implementing the recommendations provided in this chapter, higher education institutions can create more inclusive, equitable, and supportive learning environments that foster an explicit sense of belonging and empowerment for all students, drawing upon the lessons learned from the HBCU experience.

References

Al-Azawei, A., Serenelli, F. and Lundqvist, K. (2016) Universal Design for Learning (UDL): A Content Analysis of Peer-Reviewed Journal Papers from 2012 to 2015. Journal of the Scholarship of Teaching and Learning, 16, 39-56. https://doi.org/10.14434/josotl.v16i3.19295

Baker III, F. W. (2017). An alternative approach: Openness in education over the last 100 years. *TechTrends*, *61*(2), 130–140.

Bennett College. (2021). Commencement 2021 [YouTube Video]. In *YouTube*. https://www.youtube.com/watch?v=mW7NXGcuIBo

Bridges, B. K., Kinzie, J., Nelson Laird, T. F., & Kuh, G. D. (2008). Student engagement and student success at historically Black and Hispanic-serving institutions. In M. Gasman, B. Baez, & C. S. V. Turner (Eds.), Understanding minority-serving institutions (pp. 217–236). State University of New York Press.

Brotherton, B., & Wood, R. C. (2010). Hospitality and hospitality management. In C. Lashley & A. Morrison (Eds.), *In search of hospitality* (pp. 134–156). Routledge. https://www.sciencedirect.com/science/article/abs/pii/B9780750654319500123

Burmicky, J., Rzucidlo, K., Muñoz, N., Servance, W., & Thornton, M. (2022). Mattering and belonging: An HBCU case study exploration of campus involvement during the pandemic. *Journal of Negro Education*, *91*(3), 309–321.

Chan, S. (2010). Applications of andragogy in multi-disciplined teaching and learning. *Journal of Adult Education*, *39*(2), 25–35. https://files.eric.ed.gov/fulltext/EJ930244.pdf

Chu, Z. (2016). *The first year experience on an urban campus: A case study exploring the impact of first year programs on student perceptions of belonging, adjustment, success, and support* (Doctoral dissertation), Georgia State University. https://doi.org/10.57709/8559678

FAMUTube1887. (2023). FAMU SPRING 2023 COMMENCEMENT|TMCF President & CEO Harry Williams, Ph.D.| [YouTube Video]. In *YouTube*. https://www.youtube.com/watch?v=Bh2X5e9loM8

Fink, L. D. (2005). Creating significant learning experiences: An integrated approach to designing college courses. *Journal of Chemical Education*, *82*(6), 819.

Gay, G. (2018). *Culturally responsive teaching: Theory, research, and practice*. Teachers College Press.

Harrison, E., & Thomas, M. (2021). Adaptive survival strategies: A case study analysis of four historically Black colleges and universities. In C. C.

Dawson (Ed.), *Reimagining historically Black colleges and universities* (pp. 97–108). Emerald Publishing Limited.

Hsieh, H. F., & Shannon, S. E. (2005). Three approaches to qualitative content analysis. *Qualitative Health Research, 15*(9), 1277–1288.

Johnson, J. M., & McGowan, B. L. (2017). Untold stories: The gendered experiences of high achieving African American male alumni of historically Black colleges and universities. *Journal of African American Males in Education (JAAME), 8*(1), 23–44.

Johnson, J. M., & Winfield, J. D. (2022). Institutionalizing success: Practices and policies at HBCUs that promote student development and degree attainment. *The Journal of Higher Education, 93*(7), 989–1011.

Lee, J., & Fogle, E. (2020, November 10). Diverse representation: Learner impacts and strategies in online courses. *Coursera Blog.* https://blog.coursera.org/diverse-representation-learner-impacts- andstrategies-in-online-courses/

Neuendorf, K. A. (2002). *The content analysis guidebook.* Sage.

North Carolina A&T (2024). The Undergraduate Ceremony 2: Saturday, May 11, 2024 at 2 p.m. [YouTube Video]. In *YouTube.* https://www.youtube.com/watch?v=iTNPxnRCUeQ

Özturgut, O. (2017). Internationalization for diversity, equity, and inclusion. *Journal of Higher Education Theory & Practice, 17*(6), 83–91. https://www.researchgate.net/publication/322804711 _Internationalization_for_Diversity_Equity_and_Inclusion

Palmer, R., & Gasman, M. (2008). "It takes a village to raise a child": The role of social capital in promoting academic success for African American men at a Black college. *Journal of College Student Development, 49*(1), 52–70.

Rasheed, M. A., Shahzad, K., Conroy, C., Nadeem, S., & Siddique, M. U. (2017). Exploring the role of employee voice between high-performance work system and organizational innovation in small and medium enterprises. *Journal of Small Business and Enterprise Development, 24*(4), 670–688.

Schwitzer, A., Griffin, O. T., Ancis, J. R., & Thomas, C. R. (1999). Social adjustment experiences of African American college students. *Journal of Counseling and Development, 77*(2), 189–197.

Strayhorn, T. L. (2019). *College students' sense of belonging: A key to educational success for all students.* Routledge.

Strayhorn, T. L. (2020). Measuring the relation between sense of belonging, campus leadership, and academic achievement for African American students at historically Black colleges and universities (HBCUs): A "gender equity" analysis. *Journal of Minority Achievement, Creativity, and Leadership*, *1*(1), 94–118.

Strayhorn, T. L. (2023). Widening the aperture on college students' sense of belonging: A critical ecological perspective. In J. A. Hunn & T. L. Strayhorn (Eds.), *Advancing student engagement in higher education* (pp. 251–261). Routledge.

Thomas, M., Harris, R., & King-Berry, A. (2017). Creating inclusive online learning environments that build community and enhance learning. In L. Kyei-Blankson, E. Ntuli, & J. Blankson (Eds.), Handbook of research on innovative pedagogies and technologies for online learning in higher education (pp. 1–21). IGI Global.

Thomas, M., & Thomas, S. W. (2023). Leveraging the WHOLE experience framework to elevate inclusive learning. *Journal of Educational Research and Practice*, *12*, 10.

Toldson, I. A., & Cooper, G. (2014). istorically Black colleges and universities data dashboard (pp. 1–10). US Department of Education, White House Initiative on Historically Black Colleges and Universities.

Williams, J., Ashley, D., & Rhea, S. (2004). *I'll find a way or make one: A tribute to historically black colleges and universities*. Amistad.

Williams, K. L., Russell, A., & Summerville, K. (2021). Centering blackness: An examination of culturally-affirming pedagogy and practices enacted by HBCU administrators and faculty members. *Innovative Higher Education*, *46*, 733–757.

Yavorski, K. (2019, October). *Your typical college student has changed–why haven't college policies*. Higher Education Leadership, Inc.

Zimmerman, M. A. (2000). Empowerment theory. In J. Rappaport & E. Seidman (Eds.), *Handbook of community psychology* (pp. 43–63). Springer.

9

Black College Men with Disabilities Involvement On- and Off-Campus

Critical Insights for Policy, Practice, and Future Research

Terrell L. Strayhorn and J'Quen O. Johnson

Chapter Outline

Introduction

Diversity is a hallmark of American higher education reflected in the various institutions and students that comprise the system, as I've alluded in earlier writings. Consider that there are over 4,300 colleges and universities in the United States (US). Over half of these are open-access 2-year community colleges, approximately 260 research universities, 600 liberal arts colleges, and 101 Historically Black Colleges and Universities (HBCUs) (Carnegie Foundation for the Advancement of Teaching, 2000). Institutional diversity is further complicated by student demographic differences. Recent data from the US Department of Education (2022) indicates that there are approximately twenty million college students today, the vast majority of them being women, over one-third first-generation or *first in their family to attend college*, 45 percent racial/ethnic minorities, and 21 percent with disabilities.

College students with disabilities face myriad challenges. Challenges include low expectations among faculty/staff, inaccessible campus facilities, difficulty requesting academic accommodations, and managing disability stigma, to name a few (Hong, 2015). Disability stigma often stems from a lack of understanding or support from faculty, staff, and peers, that's all too frequently rooted in ableist assumptions and beliefs. Ableism is a system of discrimination and prejudice that privileges non-disabled individuals while marginalizing those with disabilities. By disabilities, we refer to physical or mental impairment or medical conditions that significantly impact daily functioning (ADA, 2024; Fuentes et al., 2023).

Prior research suggests that other social identities shape the experiences of college students with disabilities. For instance, Black college men with disabilities navigate hostile educational environments where they are bullied, called names, labeled, and discredited about their disability status (Eisenman et al., 2020). Additionally, previous studies have shown that 83 percent of freshman Black men report mental health disabilities (Williams et al., 2023) and disabled Black college men are more likely than others to feel judged, have their competence questioned, and encounter pejorative stereotypes that lead non-Black faculty and peers to assume their disability is the result of gun violence, not innate medical conditions. Interestingly, Black college men with visible and invisible disabilities agreed that social identities shape their experiences but disagreed on which factor contributed most (Banks & Hughes, 2013). Nevertheless, they judge predominantly white and ableist higher education environments as generally unwelcoming, unsupportive, and uninviting, which reduces, if not inhibits, their involvement in college. Involvement refers to the frequency and nature of students' investment of physical and psychological energy in college activities (Astin, 1984).

Contrary to popular belief, college students with disabilities are involved in campus activities according to previous studies (e.g., Kimball et al., 2017). Far less is known about the on- and off-campus involvement of Black college men with disabilities, despite few exceptions (Strayhorn & Johnson, 2024). What little is known clearly suggests that Black college men with disabilities *are involved* on campus and beyond, although the frequency and nature of their involvement may not resemble that of their same-race, able-bodied peers (Strayhorn & Johnson). The study that informs the present chapter addresses the underexplored gap that remains in terms of disabled Black college men's involvement.

Purpose

The purpose of this chapter is to highlight evidence-based insights about the on- and off-campus involvement of Black college men with disabilities, based on data from our previous studies with such students (e.g., Strayhorn & Johnson, 2023, 2024). A single question guided the investigation: What role does *disability* play in the on- and off-campus involvement of Black college men with disabilities? Drawing on data from mostly qualitative interview-based projects, we sought to investigate and understand campus involvement from the perspectives of Black college men with disabilities. Before defining the chapter's theoretical framework, we briefly review the extant literature in the next section.

Brief Literature Review

Research on college students with disabilities is growing, yet still fairly limited. It can be organized into three major categories. First, previous scholars have examined the experiences of disabled college students on campus. For example, Hong (2015) used reflective journaling to collect data from sixteen undergraduates with disabilities at a small suburban school on the East Coast. Four barriers affect their involvement. Students avoid revealing accommodation needs to instructors for fear of being treated differently or feeling embarrassed, humiliated, and prejudged. Academic advisors seem to lack care for students as individuals, and advising incompetence limited students' success. Daily life stressors such as side effects from medications, emotional/mental challenges, and disability stigma lead to other frustrations that compromise their involvement in the academic and social spheres of college life.

Often adopting an intersectional perspective, education- and disability scholars have examined the academic and social experiences of Black college students with disabilities. Walker and Test (2011) conducted a qualitative study to evaluate the effects of a self-advocacy intervention program on academically oriented behaviors for three African American college men with disabilities. Analyzing data from multiple sources, they found that students rated the intervention as effective in helping them use advocacy skills to request accommodations. Additionally, all students described how the intervention positively influenced their ability to learn and engage on campus. For example, the intervention helped Alex describe how ADHD made it difficult to pay attention in class or easily distracted him when other students were talking. While useful, results seem to place enormous responsibility on the student, representing a form of a second curriculum they must master in addition to other academic requirements.

Those who study Black college men with disabilities typically emphasize the influence of disability labels on negative stereotype threat and the role racially affirming campus environments play in their academic success (Banks & Hughes, 2013), giving short shrift to their involvement experiences. For instance, Banks and Hughes studied twelve African American college men "labeled with" disabilities at a 4-year HBCU located in the Mid-Atlantic region of the United States to explore their academic experiences and perspectives (p. 371). Analyzing data from semi-structured phenomenological interviews, they found that Black men in the study report awareness of disability as a marginalized cultural status that raises questions about their competence. Students construct individual counternarratives to serve as a psychological defense against negative stereotypes and dominant scripts. Men in their study also benefit from the racially affirming, nurturing environment that HBCUs provide for Black students. Specifically, they spoke at length about helpful staff, supportive faculty who offer accommodations, and disability support specialists who go beyond the call of duty to best support their academic and social involvement.

Taken together, empirical findings point to the importance of disability, the influence of campus environments, and the distinct experiences of Black men with disabilities. Studies are needed that explore the involvement experiences of Black men with disabilities in college. Before describing our study, we review the lens that shapes our qualitative examination.

Theoretical Framework

Critical Disability Theory (CDT) serves as the theoretical framework for this study, providing a lens to examine the lived experiences of disabled Black college men and their involvement on- and off-campus. CDT extends beyond the medical and social models of disability to interrogate how power structures, societal norms, and institutional logics and practices marginalize or "disable" disabled individuals. At its core, CDT challenges the assumption that disability is an inherent deficit or deviation from normalcy. Instead, it views disability on a continuum as a social, cultural, and political construct that emerges through interactions between individuals and disabling environments.

There are several core tenets of CDT. They include critique of normalcy, social and environmental barriers, and intersectionality, to name three that undergird our analysis. Critique of normalcy involves questioning the dominance of ableist standards that frame able-bodiedness as the norm and disability as a deviation. Social and environmental barriers shift the focus from individual impairments and limitations to systemic and environmental conditions that create disability. Lastly, intersectionality emphasizes how disability intersects with other identities, such as race, gender, and socioeconomic status, to shape relatively unique experiences of oppression and privilege.

In prior disability studies, CDT has been instrumental in highlighting the intersection of disability and race, particularly the unique challenges faced by disabled individuals of color. For example, CDT has been used to critique the inequities in education systems that disproportionately label students of color as having disabilities while failing to provide adequate support (Abes & Wallace, 2018). It has also informed analyses of employment discrimination and access to public spaces, illustrating how policies and practices reinforce systemic ableism and racism (Fuentes et al., 2023). Interestingly, to our knowledge, CDT has *neither* been used to "give voice" to the experiences of Black college men who are deaf, mute, or neurodiverse, nor to speak to the "lived experiences" of those who can't see, can't feel, or can't speak with their mouths, but rather with hands (i.e., ASL) or digitized voices.

In this study, CDT provides a framework for examining how systemic and structural factors shape disabled Black college men's experiences and opportunities for involvement on- and off-campus. By focusing on environmental barriers, institutional policies, and societal norms, this study seeks to uncover the ways ableism and racism interact to influence these students' engagement, in ways that truly advance what's known from contemporary research about college student involvement. CDT's commitment to centering marginalized voices ensures that the perspectives of disabled Black men are at the forefront, offering insights into how higher education and community settings can be transformed to better support belonging and success.

Methods

Given the book's focus on college student involvement, we drew upon data from an ongoing, multi-site qualitative study on Black men with disabilities at predominantly white institutions (PWIs) and HBCUs.

Data were collected via semi-structured, one-on-one, in-depth interviews with willing participants that were audio- or video-recorded. Participants were recruited in two ways. Recruitment began with digital flyers disseminated to professionals in campus disability services (CDS) offices via a listserv hosted by a four-year public institution. Listserv notifications encouraged CDS professionals to recommend eligible students for the study or forward the announcement to students registered with their office. Office-based recruitment was complemented by a broader outreach effort through collaboration with a research firm. The research firm posted invitations on static websites and launched social media campaigns targeting audiences that met the sampling criteria. Criteria-based advertisements included details about the study's purpose, scope, and instructions for enlisting in the project by contacting a member of the research team.

Data were analyzed in five stages. First, a professional transcribed one-on-one interviews using artificial intelligence (AI) technology converting audio to text. Second, the electronic transcripts were stored in qualitative data analysis software (i.e., Atlas.Ti 23) and initially analyzed using NVivo. Then, researchers conducted a line-by-line review of the transcripts, marking words and phrases relevant to the guiding question. Third, these initial words and phrases formed the basis of preliminary codes, also known as open coding. Open coding, an interpretive process for examining and categorizing raw qualitative data, was used to classify and chunk comments shared during interviews. Fourth, open coding led to axial coding, which involves connecting categories and subcategories to form larger, overarching themes. Lastly, we compared and contrasted categories, which in turn resulted in final themes that serve as major findings in this study.

Findings

Disability Complicates Student's Experiences

Data from our various studies clearly suggest that Black college men with disabilities *are involved* in college, contrary to popular belief. They are residence hall advisors, campus orientation leaders, elected student government officers, and members of predominantly Black Greek letter organizations, namely fraternities and sororities, to name just a few. However, their involvement is powerfully shaped by dominant perceptions that separate power and privilege, abled and disabled, as well as normal and abnormal. For instance, Black men in our studies spoke about how their disability status served as a "scarlet letter" of sorts, that doomed them to always be seen as an invalid not capable, deserving, or qualified.

Disability also influences the frequency and nature of Black college men's involvement on- and off-campus. For example, Black guys in our studies talked at length about being involved in discipline-based organizations, such as Future Business Leaders of America or National Society of Black Engineers, but often constricted their involvement to less visible, "behind the scenes" roles such as social media manager, treasurer, or webmaster that shielded them from the hurt, harm, and pain of teasing, bullying, or name-calling. Others talked about being involved in off-campus mentoring programs, church groups, and creative arts societies that satisfy their need for community, but directed their energies off-campus, not on campus.

Whether involved on- or off-campus, our guys stressed the level of care and concern that people showed toward their involvement. It was when peers went out of their way to create or hold space for them to share their ideas or air their concerns that made a difference. It was when faculty checked in on them when they missed class that Black men in our studies knew they mattered, were "more than a number" on a roster, and truly belonged. It was when the off-campus Bible study leaders added them to the group chat that made them feel important, significant, and a bona fide member of the group, with all rights and privileges afforded thereto. Although comments reveal how disability complicates involvement experiences at the individual level, they also speak to the role of environmental factors.

Social Environments Disable Involvement

CDT underscores how social environments interact with systemic ableism to negatively impact disabled Black college men. Social environments extend beyond physical spaces to include institutional practices, campus cultures, and interpersonal dynamics. Black men in our studies recounted navigating classrooms, student organizations, and residence halls that reinforced and reified feelings of social and psychological exclusion. Exclusion often manifested in subtle yet devastating ways, such as professors refusing accommodations due to incomplete paperwork or student affairs program coordinators overlooking accessibility needs. These men were clear: their marginalization wasn't incidental but a predictable outcome of environments designed without their basic involvement needs in mind, especially when they differed significantly from their more able-bodied peers.

Attitudes and behaviors from faculty, staff, and peers within these social environments on- and off-campus further compound their challenges. Black men described experiences where faculty, staff, and peers display a lack of understanding about their disabilities, often rooted in ableist assumptions. For example, one guy shared a story about an on campus event held at a venue that was difficult to access for people like him who used a wheelchair. Despite voicing his concerns, staff seemed to downplay the issue and minimize the matter, leaving him feeling like an "unwelcomed afterthought." Others detailed how their requests for accommodations, such as extended test time or mental health-related absences, were often met with skepticism or outright rejection, especially by white faculty/staff. Skepticism and denial were often accompanied by comments implying they were lazy or unfit for college.

Disability is not merely an individual experience; it's shaped by environments that either enable or disable participation in college life. Active participation in higher education spaces should foster belonging (Strayhorn, 2019), yet many of these men encountered environments that stripped them of agency and autonomy. Black men with mental health challenges, for instance, noted how deadlines and rigid academic policies ignored their realities of navigating depressive episodes or anxiety attacks. One student recounted a particularly grueling semester where his request to reschedule an exam due to a severe panic attack was denied. His professor was unwilling to grant an extension based on the faulty common-belief that: "If an exception is made for you, I have to do it for everyone." This clearly seems to miss that not every student battles anxiety, depressive episodes, and mental health disabilities like our participants. Lack of flexibility and empathy not only hindered Black college men's academic success in our studies but also deepened their feelings of insignificance, invisibility, or isolation.

Isolation breeds frustration, and frustration eventually erodes involvement. Black men in our studies highlighted how repeated experiences of feeling overlooked or dismissed led them to pull away from opportunities for building trusting relationships with faculty/staff and connecting with peers on campus. For some, this meant skipping class or campus events, especially those held in buildings or spaces that were difficult to access for people with mobility restrictions (e.g., wheelchair, limp, or uneven walking pattern) or dimly lit for those with visual impairments. For others, it meant avoiding icebreakers, social receptions, or declining campus leadership roles due to fears of being judged or misunderstood because of a speech impairment (e.g., stuttering) or physical deformity. If nothing else, we learned that involvement is shaped by multiple factors for the men in our studies.

Involvement Shaped by Intersectional Identities

Intersectionality, a core tenet of CDT, reveals how layered social identities interact to create specific barriers to involvement. Black college men in our studies shared stories of feeling hypervisible as Black men but invisible as individuals with disabilities. Hypervisibility manifested in classrooms, where faculty scrutinized their behaviors and judged them more harshly than their differently abled peers, labeling them as lazy when accommodations were requested. Simultaneously, their disabilities were rendered invisible in campus-wide diversity efforts that prioritized race or gender without considering how disability intersects with these identities. One student shared his experience as a member of both the Black Student Union and the Disability Cultural Center, noting how each group acknowledged only parts of his identity. While the Black Student Union embraced his Blackness, it seemed to disregard disabilities by throwing Black History Month parties on rooftops that offer limited access to those with mobility issues or hosting gatherings with intense strobe lights that overstimulate the autistic or distract those with ADHD. Conversely, the Disability Cultural Center celebrated his disability but largely ignored racial identity by only inviting white disabled speakers for major events or avoiding conversations about the role of race and racism within the disabled community.

Their experiences of intersectionality also shaped how they perceived and accessed opportunities for involvement. Black men often felt pressure to downplay their disability in spaces designed to celebrate student leadership or excellence. Excellence, as they described, was all too often equated with able-bodied norms such as speaking up for oneself and "walking the walk," which can be difficult for those who speak with their hands or walk with a mobility aid. Black men in our interviews shared how they avoided disclosing their disabilities in leadership roles, fearing they would be deemed incompetent or unworthy of full-fledged membership. Intersecting identities also shaped how Black men with disabilities evaluated the risks and benefits of involvement. Risks of being misjudged or ostracized often outweighed the potential benefits of participating in campus life. Moments of exclusion, shaped by intersecting stereotypes about race and disability, diminished their desire to engage, leaving them isolated from peers and disconnected from campus resources.

Discussion

Recall that the purpose of this study was to investigate and understand on- and off-campus involvement of Black college men with disabilities. A single question guided the project: What role does *disability* play in the on- and off-campus involvement of Black college men with disabilities? Findings suggest a number of important conclusions. Our first major finding reveals that disability complicates Black college men's involvement experiences. Disabled Black college men constricted their involvement to less visible leadership roles to protect themselves from bullying, teasing, or name-calling. To our knowledge, this represents an original finding in the research literature, one that breaks new ground on the topic and sets a strong foundation for future replication.

Our second finding affirms a major tenet of CDT that social environments "disable" Black disabled college men's involvement (Abes & Wallace, 2018). Black disabled men's involvement was limited by faculty who failed to give accommodations due to inadequate paperwork. Student affairs program coordinators, on the other hand, often overlooked accessibility needs, in keeping with other studies. So, it's not so much the medical condition that negatively impacted the guys in our studies, but everyday policies and practices that disabled their ability to be involved and successful in college.

Our third major finding aligns with another core tenet of CDT: social identities intersect and simultaneously influence phenomena. The involvement of Black college men with disabilities is profoundly shaped by their intersectional identities, as race, gender, and disability converge to influence how they engage within higher education. Higher education environments often compartmentalize student identities, failing to acknowledge how overlapping forms of oppression and privilege uniquely shape experiences. For Black men with disabilities, their race is rarely separable from their disability, and neither exists outside the context of societal stereotypes about race. Race frequently clashes with the vulnerabilities of living with a disability, creating an internal and external tug-of-war that limits their ability to fully engage on- and off-campus. Results call for creating inclusive campus programs that honor the multifaceted nature of identity, from race and gender to disability and beyond. They also call for rejecting one-size-fits-all approaches to diversity that erase the unique challenges of intersectional identities for Black college men with disabilities.

Findings from this study highlight important implications for policies, practices, and research that aim to support and enhance the involvement of Black college men with disabilities. First, institutions must adopt policies that intentionally foster inclusive involvement opportunities. Policymakers might consider creating funding streams specifically allocated to support involvement programs for underrepresented student populations. For example, campuses could establish involvement grants that offset the financial and logistical barriers to participating in student organizations, leadership programs, or off-campus community service initiatives and non-partisan religious groups. Such policies would not only expand access to involvement opportunities but also signal a commitment to equity and inclusion in higher education.

Student affairs professionals can play a pivotal role by designing involvement programs that integrate accessibility and cultural responsiveness using concepts from universal design for learning (UDL). Programs such as leadership academies or community service initiatives could intentionally incorporate accommodations and build in spaces for students to discuss how their intersecting identities shape their involvement experiences. For instance, hosting disability-inclusive leadership retreats that include affinity groups like *e-Buddies* or Disabilities-R-Us for Black men with disabilities could provide safe and affirming environments to explore their roles as campus and community leaders. Additionally, offering virtual involvement options such as art groups, e-sports, or *Fortnite* and *Madden* gaming clubs could remove barriers for Black college men who experience challenges with face-to-face sociability, mobility, or transportation, while also facilitating connections between them and their same-race and/or differently abled peers.

Disability support services might collaborate with student activities staff to create more accessible involvement opportunities. This could involve training student leaders on inclusive practices, such as providing meeting materials in multiple formats or ensuring physical accessibility in event planning. Creating direct partnerships between disability services and student organizations could also be effective. For example, information, statistics, and promising practices can be prominently displayed on CDS websites and social media that are highly trafficked by students. CDS might also sponsor student-led advocacy groups focused on addressing ableism and fostering a sense of belonging for disabled students of color.

Faculty can support involvement by encouraging connections between academic coursework and extracurricular activities. Integrating involvement into academic experiences—such as assigning group projects that require collaboration with student organizations or encouraging participation in academic clubs—can help Black men with disabilities find new pathways to engagement. Faculty mentorship can also play a critical role in connecting students with on- and off-campus opportunities that align with their strengths and interests.

Finally, future research should explore the various ways that Black men with disabilities navigate and define involvement in higher education. While much of the existing literature focuses on traditional measures of campus engagement using qualitative methods in the US, future studies could investigate how students in the United States or abroad conceptualize involvement within and beyond campus boundaries using quantitative metrics, large-scale datasets, and locally constructed surveys. For example, scholars might examine the roles of family, church, and community organizations in facilitating off-campus involvement of disabled Black men. Research could also explore how institutional practices such as Disability Cultural Centers, intrusive advising, or faculty-student mentoring influence the frequency and nature of involvement for these students, particularly at HBCUs and PWIs using information from the *National Survey of Student Engagement* (NSSE), *College Student Experiences Questionnaire* (CSEQ), or *Trends in International Mathematics and Science Study* (TIMSS), where possible.

Conclusion

Black college men with disabilities are involved in activities on- and off-campus. They are actively involved in clubs, organizations, and fraternities, although they limit their role to less visible positions to avoid ridicule, harm, and pain. Medical conditions matter, but social environments also disable Black college men's involvement in significant ways. If nothing else, we learned that not all disabled Black college men are the same—they experience involvement differently based on the unique convergence of social identities that make them *who* they are. So, friends, let's use this information to fashion campus conditions where they can truly thrive, flourish, and feel a sense of belonging free from the pain of negative labels like "dumb," "stupid," "lazy," and "invalid," which have left deep wounds in far too many. To do anything less would not only be uncivil, but uncivilized. And they deserve better than that.

References

Abes, E. S., & Wallace, M. M. (2018). "People see me, but they don't see me": An intersectional study of college students with physical disabilities. *Journal of College Student Development*, *59*(5), 545–562. https://dx.doi.org/10.1353/csd.2018.0052.

ADA National Network. (2024, December 12). *What is the definition of disability under the ADA?*. https://adata.org/faq/what-definition-disability-under-ada

Astin, A. W. (1984). Student involvement: A developmental theory for higher education. *Journal of College Student Personnel*, *25*, 297–308.

Banks, J., & Hughes, M. S. (2013). Double consciousness: Postsecondary experiences of African American males with disabilities. *The Journal of Negro Education*, *82*(4), 368–381. https://doi.org/10.7709/jnegroeducation.82.4.0368

Carnegie Foundation for the Advancement of Teaching. (2000). *A classification of institutions of higher education*. Author

Eisenman, L. T., Rolón-Dow, R., Freedman, B., Davison, A., & Yates, N. (2020). "Disabled or not, people just want to feel welcome": Stories of microaggressions and microaffimations from college students with intellectual disability. *Critical Education*, *11*(17), 1–12.

Fuentes, K., Hsu, S., Patel, S., & Lindsay, S. (2023). More than just double discrimination: A scoping review of the experiences and impact of ableism and racism in employment. *Disability and Rehabilitation*, *46*(4), 650–671. https://doi.org/10.1080/09638288.2023.2173315

Hong, B. S. (2015) Qualitative analysis of the barriers college students with disabilities experience in higher education. *Journal of College Student Development*, *56*, 209–226.

Kimball, E., Friedensen, R. E., & Silva, E. (2017). Engaging disability: Trajectories of involvement for college students with disabilities. In E. Kim & K. C. Aquino (Eds.), *Disability as diversity in higher education* (pp. 61–74). Routledge.

Strayhorn, T. L. (2019). *College students' sense of belonging: A key to educational success for all students* (2nd ed.). Routledge.

Strayhorn, T. L., & Johnson, J. O. (2024). A national investigation of sense of belonging among Black adult learners living with learning disabilities. *Social Education Research*, 5(2), 421–432.

Strayhorn, T. L., & Johnson, J. O. (2023). "It's bad enough I'm Black . . . But disabled too?!": A qualitative exploration of after-Covid-19 experiences for black college men living with disabilities. *Youth*, *3*(3), 1063–1077.

U.S. Department of Education, National Center for Education Statistics. (2022). *The condition of education 2021 (NCES 2022).* U.S. Government Printing Office.

Walker, A. R., & Test, D. W. (2011). Using a self-advocacy intervention on African American college students' ability to request academic accommodations. *Learning Disabilities Research & Practice, 26*(3), 134–144.

Williams, K. D. A., Adkins, A., Kuo, S. I., LaRose, J. G., Utsey, S. O., Guidry, J. P. D., Spit for Science Working Group, Dick, D., & Carlyle, K. E. (2023). Mental health disorder symptom prevalence and rates of help-seeking among University-Enrolled, emerging adults. *Journal of American College Health*, *71*(1), 61–68. https://doi.org/10.1080/07448481.2021.1873791

Epilogue

The Future Is Belonging

Chapter Outline

As we close this exploration of belonging and involvement in higher education, one thing is crystal clear: we're not just talking about nice-to-have campus experiences. We're talking about the very foundation of student success, personal transformation, and educational equity. The stories, data, and insights shared throughout these pages paint a compelling picture of what's possible when colleges and universities take belonging seriously.

Textbook definitions suggest that an *epilogue* is a commentary or speech about what has happened or transpired. In keeping with such explanations, this *Epilogue* serves several major purposes. First, to restate the purpose and scope of this book, *Sense of Belonging and Involvement in College*. Second, the chapter will briefly review the main contents of the volume—that is, chapter summaries of what this incredible cast of scholars has offered to further advance our understanding of campus involvement and the pivotal role it plays in boosting students' sense of belonging. Third, dominant themes and conclusions flow from the book's chapters into a stream of general conclusions and recommendations for future policy, practice, and research. A final section of the *Epilogue* serves as a "speech" of sorts—a closing keynote, in written form, that paves the way forward for the next generation of scholarship that addresses the nexus between involvement and belonging. Let's go!

Where We've Been, Where We're Going

Sense of Belonging and Involvement in College presents riveting information from data-driven chapters by leading scholars and practitioners that uncover and affirm a sense of belonging as vital for student success, revealing how deep involvement catalyzes such connections. This book offers valuable insights for educators and students alike, emphasizing the transformative power of campus involvement, community, and connections in higher education.

Sense of Belonging and Involvement in College is a comprehensive exploration of the essential role involvement plays in fostering belonging to ensure student success within higher education. The book is structured around data-based chapters, each packed with evidence from empirical studies that illuminate how academic and social experiences can significantly impact a strong sense of belonging and vice versa.

The opening chapters laid the groundwork by defining belonging and student involvement, especially their importance in the college environment. Through candid discussion of findings from various studies, the book highlights how students who feel connected to their peers and institutions through formal and informal means of involvement are more likely to excel academically and persist in their studies. It emphasizes that belonging is not just a feel-good concept; it's a critical component that shapes educational outcomes, largely through student involvement in academic and social experiences, in keeping with prior work (Strayhorn, 2019).

Subsequent chapters dove deeper into the mechanisms by which involvement facilitates belonging. The book details how participation in extracurricular activities (Chapter 2 and 7), identity-based athletics (Chapter 3), minority-serving institutions (Chapter 4 and 8), social organizations, spiritual/secular spaces (Chapter 6), and service learning (Chapter 5) can create opportunities for students to forge meaningful connections, play important roles, and feel a sense of belonging in college. Each chapter provides solid practical recommendations for practice, programs, and policy, enabling educators and administrators to implement strategies that nurture inclusivity and engagement.

Moreover, the book addresses diverse student populations, discussing how different identities and backgrounds can influence sense of belonging. It offers insights into creating supportive environments that cater to the unique needs of all students, ensuring that no one feels marginalized. Candid discussions encourage readers to critically reflect on their own practices and the institutional structures that can either hinder or promote belonging.

Sense of Belonging and Involvement in College also serves as both a scholarly resource and a practical guide. It equips educators, administrators, and students with the tools to cultivate a thriving campus culture where everyone feels valued and connected. By bridging research and practice, this book underscores that creating a sense of belonging and involvement is not just beneficial—it is essential for creating successful educational experiences in college.

From Generation Covid's resilience in maintaining connections during unprecedented isolation to Black LGBTQ+ student-athletes navigating complex intersectional identities, from the nuanced dynamics of social class at HBCUs to the power of interfaith communities in fostering inclusion—this book has taken us on a journey through the multifaceted landscape of collegiate belonging.

> "Disabled students are very much involved, but certain aspects of campus environments disabled them from fully participating on- and off-campus."

This observation from my chapter with Johnson on Black college men with disabilities captures something profound: belonging isn't just about participation—it's about creating environments where every student can show up authentically and thrive completely. It's about building spaces where all students can feel safe, secure, and whole.

The research presented here demolishes any lingering notion that belonging is soft or secondary. Instead, it reveals belonging as the secret sauce that transforms campus involvement from mere activity into meaningful engagement, from going through the motions into genuine growth and connection.

The Belonging Revolution

What we're witnessing isn't just an evolution in higher education and student affairs practice—it's a revolution in how we think about education itself. The book's organizing framework presented in the *Introduction* reminds us that truly effective educational environments must be welcoming, holistic, open, and liberating. These aren't just buzzwords; they're blueprints for transformation and belonging (Strayhorn & Johnson, 2025).

> "Student organizations are a critical pathway to belonging but must be supported through intentional, equity-focused policies."

This insight gets to the heart of our challenge and opportunity. Campus involvement has always been powerful, but we now understand that its impact is conditional—shaped by who students are, what institutions they attend, and how intentionally we design these experiences.

A Call to Action: Recommendations for Moving Forward

The chapters in this book do more than illuminate problems—they point us toward solutions. But transformation requires more than good intentions; it demands systematic change across every level of higher education. From boardrooms to residence halls, from faculty meetings to student organization gatherings, we must reimagine how we create and sustain belonging.

The most significant barrier to belonging isn't individual bias or isolated incidents—it's the absence of institutional infrastructure designed to measure, support, and continuously improve students' sense of connection. Too many colleges operate on assumptions rather than evidence when it comes to belonging, treating it as an unmeasurable feeling rather than a quantifiable outcome that can be strategically enhanced. Thus, I put forth this list of policy recommendations.

Policy Recommendations

1. **Develop comprehensive belonging assessment protocols** that measure not just participation rates but quality of engagement across different student populations
2. **Create funding mechanisms** that specifically support programming for multiply marginalized students and intersectional identity development
3. **Establish institutional belonging officers** who coordinate campus-wide efforts to foster inclusive environments
4. **Mandate belonging-centered training** for all staff and faculty who work directly with students
5. **Implement data collection systems** that track belonging outcomes alongside traditional success metrics

These policy changes represent more than administrative adjustments—they signal a fundamental shift in institutional priorities. When campus leaders invest in belonging officers and mandate training, they're declaring that connection and inclusion aren't optional extras but core educational outcomes. When they create dedicated funding for holistic programming, they're acknowledging that traditional approaches often miss the mark for students with multiple marginalized identities.

Yet policy without practice is merely paperwork. The real work of facilitating belonging happens in the daily interactions between students and the communities they're trying to join. This is where the insights from chapter contributors become most powerful, offering concrete strategies for transforming involvement opportunities into belonging experiences.

Consider the lessons from Generation Covid: students who learned to maintain connection despite physical distance, who found creative ways to engage when traditional methods failed. Their resilience teaches us that belonging isn't location-dependent—it's *relationship-dependent.* This understanding must reshape how we design every program, every organization, every opportunity for student engagement. I present five recommendations for practice.

Practice Recommendations

1. **Design involvement opportunities** that explicitly address the needs of Generation Covid and future cohorts shaped by global disruption
2. **Center intersectionality** in all programming, recognizing that students don't leave parts of themselves at the door
3. **Create brave spaces** for difficult conversations about access, class, and privilege—even within historically inclusive institutions like HBCUs
4. **Develop mentorship programs** that connect students across identity groups while honoring the unique needs of specific populations
5. **Build accessibility into the DNA** of every program, event, and initiative from the ground up

Black LGBTQ+ student-athletes featured in this book remind us that intersectionality isn't just academic theory—it's lived reality. When we design programming that acknowledges the full complexity of students' identities, we create opportunities for authentic engagement rather than fractured participation. This means moving beyond single-identity programming toward approaches that honor the whole person.

Even our most inclusive institutions must grapple with uncomfortable truths about internal hierarchies and systemic barriers. The research on social class dynamics at HBCUs reveals that historical mission doesn't automatically translate to contemporary equity. Creating brave spaces for these conversations isn't comfortable, but it's necessary for genuine belonging, especially for students who might feel invisible, minoritized, or socially isolated at HBCUs that tend to be conservative and highly religious in nature (Harper & Gasman, 2008).

While practitioners implement new approaches, researchers must continue expanding our understanding of how belonging operates across different contexts, populations, and time periods. The pandemic offered an unexpected natural experiment in belonging, revealing both vulnerabilities and resilience we never knew existed. We cannot afford to lose these lessons as we move forward. To that end, I put forth five research recommendations to consider.

Research Recommendations

1. **Investigate long-term impacts** of pandemic-era belonging interventions on career outcomes and civic engagement
2. **Expand intersectional research** that examines how multiple identities interact to shape belonging experiences
3. **Develop culturally responsive** belonging measures that honor the diverse ways different communities experience connection
4. **Study the role of digital spaces** (e.g., artificial intelligence) in nurturing belonging for students who may be physically absent from campus
5. **Examine institutional culture factors** that either support or undermine belonging efforts

The research agenda ahead is both urgent and expansive. We need longitudinal studies that track how belonging experiences shape post-graduation outcomes, helping college student educators make the case for belonging investments with concrete evidence. We need intersectional research that moves beyond single-identity analyses to understand how multiple identities interact in complex, sometimes contradictory ways.

Perhaps most importantly, we need rigorous research that is culturally responsive—measures and methods that honor the diverse ways different communities experience and express belonging. The dominant frameworks in higher education research have historically centered white, middle-class experiences. True equity requires research approaches that reflect the full spectrum of student identities and experiences.

Tools for Transformation

To support practitioners in implementing these insights, I've developed several resources: (1) a co-curricular involvement transcript template, (2) a belonging assessment rubric, (3) key discussion questions, and (4) a list of relevant online resources (see *Appendix A*).

Belonging Assessment Rubric for Campus Involvement

This rubric represents a useful heuristic for evaluating the outcomes of campus involvement, moving beyond simple participation metrics to assess the quality and depth of students' belonging experiences. In an era of increasing accountability and value-added assessment, higher education administrators must demonstrate not just that students are involved, but that involvement translates into meaningful, robust learning outcomes. This rubric is a tool that provides college student educators with a concrete and accessible framework for measuring these tangible but crucial outcomes.

Student activities professionals can use this tool to evaluate programming effectiveness and identify students who may need additional support in finding their place on campus. Academic advisors can incorporate belonging assessments into their conversations with students, helping them reflect on how co-curricular experiences complement their academic journey and *accelerate* achievement of their academic goals. Service-learning coordinators can apply this rubric to understand how community engagement creates campus connection, while residence life staff can use it to assess the impact of floor programming, residential learning communities, and hall councils on student growth and development.

The rubric's *real* strength lies in its simplicity and versatility—it can be adapted for individual student reflection, program evaluation, or institutional effectiveness (IE) assessment, providing a common language for discussing belonging across functional areas while honoring the diverse ways students experience care, connection, and college.

The Belonging Imperative

As we look toward the future of higher education, one thing is certain: campus administrators that prioritize belonging will lead institutions that thrive. Students featured in this book—from Generation Covid learners adapting to unprecedented change to Black LGBTQ+ athletes breaking barriers to first-generation students navigating elite spaces—they're not asking for special treatment. They're asking for what every human being deserves: to be seen, valued, and embraced for who they are.

> "Using the concept of 'beloved community,' we argue for a rethinking of campus resources to center equity and inclusion."

This vision of beloved community isn't utopian idealism—it's practical necessity. In an increasingly diverse and interconnected world, our colleges and universities must become laboratories for the kind of inclusive excellence our society desperately needs.

The research is clear, the strategies are proven, and the need is urgent. What remains is the will to act. The question isn't whether we can create more belonging-centered campuses—the question is whether we will.

A Closing Note: "It's Your Turn"

As you close this book and return to your work in higher education, carry with you this truth: every interaction is an opportunity to foster belonging, every program is a chance to create connection, and every policy is a possibility to build a brighter, more inclusive future.

The students are waiting. The data are compelling. The moment is now.

The future of higher education isn't just about what we teach—it's about how we make every student feel they belong. And that future starts with you. On your darkest day, remember, YOU are some students' brightest light. Shine, gentle reader, shine . . . .

> "What we're witnessing isn't just an evolution in student affairs practice—it's a revolution in how we think about education itself."

Appendix A

Table E.1 Sense of Belonging Rubric

Criterion	Developing (1)	Proficient (2)	Advanced (3)	Exemplary (4)
Connection to Community	Limited interaction with peers	Some meaningful relationships formed	Strong network of supportive relationships	Deep, lasting connections across diverse groups
Identity Integration	Struggles to bring authentic self to activities	Some comfort expressing Identity	Confidently shares identity in most contexts	Helps other integrate their identities
Sense of Mattering	Feels overlooked or unimportant	Occasionally feels values	Regularly feels appreciated	Consistently feels essential to community
Growth Mindset	Avoids challenges, fixed perspective	Willing to try new things occasionally	Embrace challenges, seeks growth	Actively pursues development, helps others grow

Appendix B

Co-Curricular Involvement Transcript Template

Student Name:____________________ Academic Year:____________________

Table E.2 Sample Co-Curricular Transcript

Activity/ Organization	Role	Duration	Key Learning Outcomes	Belonging Impact
[Example: Black Student Union]	[Member/ Officer]	[Fall 2023-Spring 2024]	[Leadership, cultural competency]	[Increased sense of racial pride and campus connection]

Reflection Questions

- Define college students sense of belonging, in your own words.
- How does involvement enhance students' sense of belonging in college?
- What skills do students develop through their involvement experiences?
- How have you contributed to students' sense of belonging on your campus in the last six months?
- What opportunities for student involvement exist on your campus? What's missing or still needs to be developed?

These questions are provided to kick-start meaningful discussions about the book. Independent readers might contemplate these questions and jot down their thoughts in a notebook, an index card, or type them into the "notes" app on a smart device. Groups of people might come together in formal book clubs, learning communities, or community dialogue sessions at professional conferences to debate authors' claims, grapple with major recommendations, and brainstorm ways to move theory into practice. Remember this: be honest, not hollow. Lean in for understanding; don't assume. Listen, don't lecture. It's a proven way to move the needle forward and facilitate a true sense of belonging.

Appendix C

Terms

Relational consistency: Refers to the ongoing, reliable presence of supportive relationships that endure over time and across contexts. It is not merely contact, but continuity—interactions that are frequent, affirming, and predictable enough to build trust and mutual regard. Within the broader frame of sense of belonging, relational consistency signals to people that they are not only seen in isolated moments, but known across time. It converts episodic connection into durable community. When students experience consistent care from faculty, staff, and peers, they are more likely to interpret the environment as stable, trustworthy, and invested in their success—conditions that heighten their sense of mattering and connectedness.

Navigational capacity: Captures students' ability to effectively move through complex institutional environments, access resources, and make meaning of systems that are often opaque, unjust, inequitable or unevenly distributed. It reflects both skill and support—the know-how to locate opportunities, decode expectations, and leverage networks to one's advantage. In the context of sense of belonging, navigational capacity is both a pathway and a product. Students who can successfully navigate institutional structures are more likely to feel competent, included, and "insider" to the system; conversely, institutions that scaffold navigation—through advising, orientation, mentoring, and clear communication—actively cultivate belonging by reducing uncertainty, leveling hierarchies, and barring exclusion.

Narrative alignment: Refers to the degree of fit between an individual's personal story—values, goals, identities—and the dominant or espoused story of the institution. It is the felt sense that "my story belongs here" and that one's presence is not an exception but an extension of the institution's purpose. Within the ecology of belonging, narrative alignment operates as an interpretive lens: students assess whether institutional messages, symbols, and practices (past, present, or future) affirm or contradict who they are and who they seek to become. When alignment is strong, students experience coherence and legitimacy; when misaligned, they may feel peripheral, captive, conflicted, or compelled to edit themselves to remain.

Identity safety cues: Verbal, behavioral, and environmental signals that communicate whether one's salient identities are recognized, respected, and protected within a given space. These cues range from representation in curriculum and staffing, to inclusive language, to policies that affirm dignity and prohibit harm. In relation to sense of belonging, identity safety cues function as immediate, perceptible indicators of whether one can show up authentically without fear of marginalization. Their presence reduces uncertainty, anxiety, and threat, while their absence can heighten vigilance and distance. In this way, identity safety cues shape the emotional and psychological conditions under which belonging is either invited or inhibited.

Together, these terms extend the conceptual architecture of Strayhorn's (2019) sense of belonging theoretical framework by naming the conditions through which belonging is built, interpreted, and sustained. They move us beyond abstract affirmation toward actionable design—clarifying how relationships, systems, stories, and signals work in concert to tell students, in ways both subtle and explicit: *you are seen, heard, and known. You can navigate this space. Your story fits, as it is. And you are safe to be who you are.*

Resources for Continued Learning

For additional tools, assessments, and best practices, visit these websites:

🔗 Belonging Resources Hub
[https://belonging.berkeley.edu/tools-and-resources]

🔗 Campus Climate Assessment Tools
[studentengagement.org/belonging-assessment]

🔗 EAB Belonging Resources
[https://eab.com/resources/resource-center/student-belonging-resource-center/]

🔗 Belonging Blogs and Articles
[https://bit.ly/DGWSOBRez]

References

Harper, S. R., & Gasman, M. (2008). Consequences of conservatism: Black male undergraduates and the politics of historically Black colleges and universities. *The Journal of Negro Education*, 336–351.

Strayhorn, T. L. (2019). *College students' sense of belonging: A key to educational success for all students* (2nd ed.). Routledge.

Strayhorn, T. L., & Johnson, J. O. (2025). A blueprint for college students' sense of belonging. *EduLedger*. https://www.theeduledger.com/opinion/article/15744068/a-blueprint-for-college-students-sense-of-bel . . . https://www.theeduledger.com/opinion/article/15744068/a-blueprint-for-college-students-sense-of-bel . . . https://www.theeduledger.com/opinion/article/15744068/a-blueprint-for-college-students-sense-of-bel . . .

Index

Note: Page numbers in *italics* refer to Figures.

About the Authors

Chapter 1

Dr. Terrell Strayhorn is Associate Provost, Interim Dean of the School of Education, and Professor of Education and Psychology at Virginia Union University, where he also serves as Director of Research in the Center for the Study of Historically Black Colleges and Universities (HBCUs). Author of fourteen books, including *College Students' Sense of Belonging: A Key to Educational Success for All Students* and co-editor of *Belonging in Higher Education*, Professor Strayhorn has published over 200 academic publications in leading sources including peer-reviewed journal articles, data-based book chapters, reviews, and reports. He resides in Houston, Texas.

Chapter 2

Gabriel Velez is Associate Professor and Developmental Psychologist in the Department of Educational Policy and Leadership (EDPL) in the College of Education at Marquette University, with a joint appointment in psychology. Dr. Velez studies identity development in adolescents and emerging adults, particularly in relation to their educational experiences, including restorative justice, peace education, the transition to college, and artificial intelligence. He also serves as the Faculty Director of the Black and Latino/a Ecosystem and Support Transition (BLEST) Hub at Marquette, and the Chair of the Faculty Research Team for the Center for Peacemaking. He received a BA in History and Literature from Harvard University, and an MA and PhD from the University of Chicago in Comparative Human Development.

Jody Jessup-Anger is Department Chair and Professor of Higher Education at Marquette University. Her research explores how collegiate environments can facilitate or impede student learning and development. Dr. Jessup-Anger is coauthor of several books, including: *Living-Learning Communities in Practice: A Guide for Creating, Maintaining, and Sustaining Programs in Higher Education* (2024), *Living-Learning Communities that Work: A Research-Based Model for Design, Delivery and Assessment* (2018), co-editor of the *New Directions for Student Services* volume: *Addressing Sexual Violence in Student Affairs and Higher Education* (2018), and co-editor of the second edition of *Maybe I Should . . . Case Studies in Ethics for Student Affairs Professionals* (2020). Dr. Jessup-Anger co-led the Elon University Center for Engaged Learning *2017–2019 Research Seminar on Residential Learning Communities*, during which she provided guidance for four multi-institutional research teams exploring different dimensions of residential learning communities. She has also provided several keynote addresses and consultation to universities on developing and sustaining living-learning communities. In 2017 and 2024, she served as scholar-in-residence for Workshop Architects, a firm specializing in the design of campus spaces.

Max Herteen is Assistant Director of Alumni Relations at Northwestern University. A Milwaukee native, he studied History, English, and French at the University of Wisconsin–Madison and later earned his master's degree in educational policy and foundations at Marquette University. At Marquette, he coauthored several research papers and helped research educational outcomes for students of color and the "Zoomer" generation that graduated high school during the Covid-19 pandemic.

Sam Nemanich PhD is a human movement neuroscientist studying the brain and its control of human movement in adults and children. Dr. Nemanich's research surrounds understanding the neural control of movement in individuals with neurological disease and injury using behavioral (kinematics, motion analysis) and neurophysiologic (EMG, EEG, and transcranial magnetic stimulation) techniques. This research will help guide the field of neurorehabilitation. He received his PhD in Movement Science from Washington University in St. Louis and completed a postdoctoral program at the University of Minnesota.

Chapter 3

Dr. Terrell Strayhorn is Associate Provost, Interim Dean of the School of Education, and Professor of Education and Psychology at Virginia Union University, where he also serves as Director of Research in the Center for the Study of Historically Black Colleges and Universities (HBCUs). Author of fourteen books, including *College Students' Sense of Belonging: A Key to Educational Success for All Students* and co-editor of *Belonging in Higher Education*, Professor Strayhorn has published over 200 academic publications in leading sources including peer-reviewed journal articles, data-based book chapters, reviews, and reports. He resides in Houston, Texas.

J'Quen O. Johnson is a PhD candidate at the University of the Cumberlands. His research interests include issues of accessibility and inclusion, as well as facilitating a sense of belonging for disabled Black men in higher education. To date, he has published over fifteen peer-reviewed publications, academic blogs, and national conference presentations. He serves as Director of Outreach and Engagement at Do Good Work. He is an editorial board member for the *Journal of Student Affairs Research and Practice.*

Chapter 4

Jorge Burmicky, PhD, is Assistant Professor of Higher Education Leadership and Policy Studies at Howard University. His research examines equity-minded leadership and capacity building in higher education, with an emphasis on minority-serving institutions (MSIs), community colleges, and broadly accessible institutions. His research also explores policies and practices that support the educational outcomes of men of color, particularly community college Latino men.

Kathleen Rzucidlo, PhD, is a proud recent graduate of the Higher Education Leadership and Policy Studies program at Howard University where she served as the lead student-PI for the ECMC Foundation funded project "HBCU Students' Basic Needs and Capacity Building:

A Multiple Case Study." Her own research focuses on a variety of topics surrounding sense of belonging, undergraduate student experiences, graduate student experiences all through the lens of HBCUs and Minority Serving Institutions (MSIs). Her true passion and dissertation focused on the racialized nature of institutional accreditation and the relationship with HBCU member institutions. Before attending Howard University, she served as an enrollment management professional and student affairs professional.

Chapter 5

Erik Malewski, PhD, is Professor of Curriculum Studies at Kennesaw State University, USA.

Genevieve Weber, PhD, LMHC, is Associate Professor of Counselor Education at Hofstra University, USA.

Katrina Alford is a PhD candidate in rural sociology and demography at the Pennsylvania State University, USA.

Christina Turner holds the position of Senior Diversity Strategist at Johns Hopkins University.

Sue Rankin, PhD, is President of Rankin Climate and a retired professor from The Pennsylvania State University.

Chapter 6

Matthew Mayhew, PhD, is the William Ray and Marie Adamson Flesher Professor of Higher Education at The Ohio State University. He has published more than seventy-five peer-reviewed articles in journals. He is also one of the coauthors of *How College Affects Students: Volume 3.*

Musbah Shaheen, PhD, is Assistant Professor of Higher Education at the University of Massachusetts Amherst.

Christa Winkler, PhD, is Assistant Professor in the Department of Educational Leadership at Mississippi State University.

Chapter 7

Dr. Krista M. Soria (she/her) is Associate Professor of Leadership and Counseling at the University of Idaho. She is a critical quantitative researcher seeking to investigate the most equitable and inclusive programmatic practices and institutional conditions to prepare students to engage in the complexities of social change. She examines how higher education institutions can create a more supportive campus climate for students from diverse backgrounds, whether programs are equitably accessible and beneficial to all students, and how we can create structural conditions to support students' development and success.

Erin Standley earned a bachelor's degree in psychology from Simpson College and an MBA degree from Rockhurst University. She is currently pursuing a PhD in education at the University of Idaho. Erin has over fifteen years of learning and development experience, including ten years in higher education with leadership roles spanning admissions, career services, adjunct teaching, and student advising in undergraduate and graduate program settings. Erin is a certified DiSC and Myers-Briggs Type Indicator practitioner and has also achieved the master practitioner designation.

Justin Braun is pursuing a PhD in education at the University of Idaho and has earned a BS in health and human development from Montana State University, and a master's in public administration from the University of Southern California. Professionally, he works in public safety with over fifteen years of experience. Prior to a career in public safety, Justin worked as a collegiate strength and conditioning coach. In each of his professional roles, he has worked as an educator and instructor with over two decades of experience in personal development. He is currently serving as the Interim Administrator for the Montana Law Enforcement Academy.

Chapter 8

Dr. Morris Thomas serves as Provost at Wiley University. Previously, he worked as a member of the Provost's Senior Leadership team at Howard University as the Assistant Provost for Digital and Online Learning and Director of the Center for Excellence in Teaching, Learning and Assessment (CETLA). He is also Associate Professor of Educational Policy & Leadership Studies and Lecturer in the Schools of Business, specializing in Project Management. Dr. Thomas has developed a conceptual framework called the E.N.H.A.N.C.E. Learning Model. This conceptual framework provides seven strategies to inform intentional course design and delivery. Dr. Thomas is also the creator of the "W.H.O.L.E. Experience Framework," a model that centers the learners' experiences. His scholarship has taken him throughout the continental United States as well as to Canada, Cuba, Germany, India, Ireland, Malawi, Puerto Rico, and South Africa. Dr. Thomas serves as an editorial board member for the Journal of African American Males in Education, the Journal of Innovative Higher Education, the American Research Journal of Humanities & Social Sciences, and as a reviewer for the International Journal of Virtual and Personal Learning Environments.

Ms. Cindy Philpot is employed by Trinity Washington University She designs and delivers training opportunities to support teaching, learning, and assessment. She assists the Assistant Provost/Director with instructional support and professional development while engaging faculty in best practices and instructional technologies. Ms. Philpot serves on various university committees, including the Faculty Advisory Committee for the College of Medicine and the Assessment Committee. She also teaches as an adjunct professor, offering courses in Computer Concepts, Ethical Considerations, and Advanced Excel. Ms. Philpot holds several Quality Matters certifications and has expertise in instructional design, creative applications, and web tools. She earned a Bachelor's in communications from Virginia Wesleyan University and a Master's in Instructional Design and Technology, along with a graduate eLearning Certificate from George Mason University. She is currently pursuing a Doctorate in Education Management at Hampton University.

Chapter 9

Dr. Terrell Strayhorn is Associate Provost, Interim Dean of the School of Education, and Professor of Education and Psychology at Virginia Union University, where he also serves as Director of Research in the Center for the Study of Historically Black Colleges and Universities (HBCUs). Author of fourteen books, including *College Students' Sense of Belonging: A Key to Educational Success for All Students* and co-editor of *Belonging in Higher Education*, Professor Strayhorn has published over 200 academic publications in leading sources including peer-reviewed journal articles, data-based book chapters, reviews, and reports. He resides in Houston, Texas.

J'Quen O. Johnson is a PhD candidate at the University of the Cumberlands. His research interests include issues of accessibility and inclusion, as well as facilitating a sense of belonging for disabled Black men in higher education. To date, he has published over fifteen peer-reviewed publications, academic blogs, and national conference presentations. He serves as Director of Outreach and Engagement at Do Good Work. He is an editorial board member for the *Journal of Student Affairs Research and Practice.*

EPILOGUE

Dr. Terrell Strayhorn is Associate Provost, Interim Dean of the School of Education, and Professor of Education and Psychology at Virginia Union University, where he also serves as Director of Research in the Center for the Study of Historically Black Colleges and Universities (HBCUs). Author of fourteen books, including *College Students' Sense of Belonging: A Key to Educational Success for All Students* and co-editor of *Belonging in Higher Education*, Professor Strayhorn has published over 200 academic publications in leading sources including peer-reviewed journal articles, data-based book chapters, reviews, and reports. He resides in Houston, Texas.